# THE SHADOW WORK WORKBOOK

*Finding and Healing Your Unconscious Self | A Journey to Self-Discovery, Boosting Self-Esteem & Mastering Your Emotions*

SOFIA VISCONTI

© Copyright 2023 - All rights reserved.

The content contained within this book may not be reproduced, duplicated, or transmitted without direct written permission from the author or the publisher.

Under no circumstances will any blame or legal responsibility be held against the publisher, or author, for any damages, reparation, or monetary loss due to the information contained within this book, either directly or indirectly.

Legal Notice:

This book is copyright protected. It is only for personal use. You cannot amend, distribute, sell, use, quote, or paraphrase any part, or the content within this book, without the consent of the author or publisher.

Disclaimer Notice:

Please note the information contained within this document is for educational and entertainment purposes only. All effort has been executed to present accurate, up-to-date, reliable, complete information. No warranties of any kind are declared or implied. Readers acknowledge that the author is not engaged in the rendering of legal, financial, medical, or professional advice. The content within this book has been derived from various sources. Please consult a licensed professional before attempting any techniques outlined in this book.

By reading this document, the reader agrees that under no circumstances is the author responsible for any losses, direct or indirect, that are incurred as a result of the use of the information contained within this document, including, but not limited to, errors, omissions, or inaccuracies.

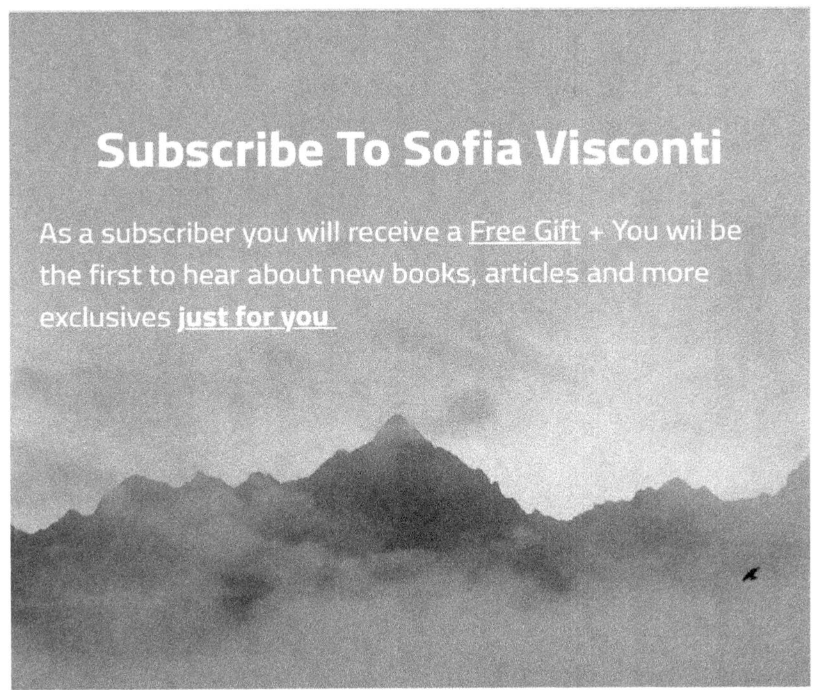

Subscribe To Sofia Visconti

As a subscriber you will receive a Free Gift + You wil be the first to hear about new books, articles and more exclusives just for you

## CLICK HERE

# CONTENTS

# INTRODUCTION

Welcome to The Shadow Work Workbook: Finding & Healing Your Unconscious Self—A Journey to Self-Discovery, Boosting Self-Esteem, & Mastering Your Emotions. All of us at Sofia Visconti are thrilled that you've chosen to embark on your journey into your shadow work. You have made a decision that will change your life forever. Your shadow uncovers secrets to the richness of life that, up until now, you may have not been able to reach. And I know your arrival to this point has not been easy. Just as Theodore Roosevelt once said,

"Nothing in the world is worth having or worth doing unless it means effort, pain, difficulty..."

And he was right. The only things worth doing in this lifetime are the challenges where you struggle, resulting in a bitter-sweet victory because you've had to battle to reach your goal. And that's the road you will take with shadow work.

Is it worth doing? Yes.

Is it going to be hard? Yes.

Have you ever had a goal or dream, but no matter how hard you tried, you couldn't make it happen? Have you wanted something so bad, but for some reason, it never worked out?

This is the effect of the shadow self. An unintegrated piece of yourself that will remain a block to many of the things you want to do in life until it is successfully integrated into your mind, body, and soul.

You see, early trauma and conditioning can create a limited version of yourself. And past experiences and trauma can affect the way you perceive the world around you.

We all have personality traits we're proud of; and we all have traits we cover up, hide, and feel embarrassed about. Those can be impulsive, toxic, and shameful, exposing ourselves as out of control, triggered, and lacking self-awareness. These are not just traits we don't feel confident about; these are aspects of our personality that throw us under the bus. So, we go to endless lengths to avoid certain people and situations, trying to hide our behavior from public view. These parts make up your shadow self, and they long to be heard.

And when you finally listen, the whole world will open up for you.

## How to Use This Workbook and Audiobook Version

Now that you are ready to begin, find a quiet space where you will be undisturbed. Light a candle and bless the space with peace and love to carry you on this journey.

Have a pen and notebook ready—a special notebook to journal and jot down things that stand out for you.

And don't forget: This workbook is designed to be used time and time again. However you traverse this journey, each time you do it, it will be very different.

If this is the first time you are using the book, certain things will be poignant depending on your current emotional state. If you decide to do the workbook again in a few months, your emotions will be different once more, and other particular features will resonate with you.

There is something to be gained every time you work through this interactive guide and undertake shadow work.

Before we begin each chapter, you are going to create a small ritual. This will help you complete the work inside this book and support you on this path.

Get ready to observe your journey and apply the following steps:

1. **Set your intention.** What do you want to achieve in each part of this workbook? What are you going to focus your efforts on? If it helps, journal on this so you can reflect on how far you've come.

2. **Take your time.** If you need to pause at any time during the workbook, please do so. Allow yourself time to think about what is coming up for you. But be mindful of getting stuck in emotions. Shadow work is deep and introspective. If you need help moving past an emotion, journal what feelings are taking over and continue with the workbook. Remember, this is a complete process—once you begin, it is important to continue to the end.

3. **Self-reflect.** Throughout the workbook, there will be places for you to pause and journal, paying attention to self-reflection. Again, give yourself time, patience, and compassion. Your truth holds the key to advancing your self-awareness; if you need time to self-reflect, take it.

4. **Journal.** This is a very important part of the workbook. Make sure you write down every thought and feeling that comes up; this helps in the process of reflection, release, and integration. Everything you feel is part of you and should not be ignored, however distressing. This will ease your journey of integration as we move forward.

5. **Seek support.** At any time during this workbook, if you feel you need to gain clarity over an emotion or ask for a second opinion—ask a friend, mentor, coach, or therapist to hold space for you, so you can share these experiences and gain insights. This can be a huge step in helping you advance further in this self-care practice and ease your challenges at the same time.

6. **Integrate.** Your shadow needs to be integrated to allow you to regain yourself and move into full physical, emotional, and spiritual alignment. Acceptance is key to integrating anything you've feared, hidden, and avoided. By integrating lost pieces of yourself, your future self will be ever-evolving. Just watch your daily life improve!

7. **Celebrate.** At the end of each chapter of the workbook, I want you to celebrate yourself. Whether that's lighting a candle on a cupcake to pat yourself on the back, buying a new outfit, or going out for dinner, mark your journey with celebratory milestones. This is a must as part of the shadow work practice you are navigating.

And don't forget, at all times, I'm with you.

## Getting Started With Shadow Work

Are you ever triggered by something? Sometimes, it can be a behavior trait that you've seen in another person. For me, beginning my shadow work was tough. I was triggered by two things: a lack of respect and inauthentic people. This followed me around for years. I couldn't look at someone who had been rude or disrespectful to me and quietly think, "That's your problem." I would explode and shout or ghost them, punishing them with the silent treatment.

When I met a seemingly fake or inauthentic person, a similar thing would happen. I could feel my toes curl, and I'd be overcome with dislike, which almost felt like hatred. Physically, I needed to exit their company almost immediately, and I'd be angry with my friends if they continued with a friendship with them. What was happening to me?

I was looking in a mirror.

These aspects of people who, to be honest, I didn't know well or care too much for, were sending me spiraling. But all they were doing was showing me pieces of myself that I disliked. And using the word "dislike" is way too gentle. They were showing me pieces of myself I couldn't stand. I hated these parts of myself that I desperately tried to cover up.

As I took a more prominent role in my work, I had to come face-to-face with more people, and I started to feel exposed. What if others noticed these things about me? I was terrified, and so my journey into my shadow work began.

So, when you ask, "Where do I start with shadow work?" the fact that you're here means you've already begun. You've yearned for change, and deep down you know that you must walk this path if you ever want to truly have fulfillment and reach your goals.

## The Importance of Self-Discovery

Self-discovery isn't just knowing who you are, it's knowing exactly what makes you tick. Emotional intelligence will get you a lot further in life than any set of qualifications will, and that's a fact. You can have all the money and the best job in the world, but if you can't regulate your emotions, or choose a partner who can regulate theirs, it's likely your life will be full of hurdles and chaos. You'll make poor choices and bad financial decisions and destroy things you've worked hard for. Sound familiar?

Why are some of the world's wealthiest people unhappy? Because they lack emotional intelligence.

So, to stop you from wondering what self-discovery is, let's look at what it encompasses so you can have a good idea of where you are on your own journey of self-discovery:

- Being in tune with your intuition, listening to your body, and feeling gut reactions

- Understanding your emotions when they come up and being able to identify why you are feeling them
- Expressing your opinions and defending yourself
- Stopping comparing yourself with others
- Setting boundaries with yourself and others
- Understanding what holds you back
- Acknowledging and understanding your fears
- Understanding when you are slipping into negative self-talk
- Developing compassion for yourself and combining it with self-love
- Identifying bad habits
- Starting to work on your bad habits because you know they don't serve you
- Setting heartfelt goals that are soul-desired and aligned
- Making a list of your strengths and weaknesses so you spend more time working with your strengths to avoid frustration
- Living intentionally in alignment with your values and belief system
- Fostering, developing, and cherishing relationships and exploring healthy new ones
- Learning from your past and forgiving yourself for the choices you made when you didn't know any better
- Looking objectively at your self-esteem, identifying where it could be improved, and accepting what you can't change
- Taking steps to work toward your ultimate dream or goal in life

How many of these can you say apply to you? Go back through the list now and check off the ones you can, making a note of the ones you want to work on, too.

## The Importance of Self-Esteem

Self-esteem controls your decision-making; it is the power that fuels your choices and affects your motivation. When self-esteem is low, it can feel like you're batting the whole world.

Your standards are built on your level of self-esteem, and low self-esteem means low standards. Let's take the example of toxic relationships. When your self-esteem is at rock bottom, you will accept having a relationship with someone disrespectful, argumentative, aggressive, or who asserts coercive control.

However, when your self-esteem is high, you don't tolerate any of these bad behaviors because you know you're worth more than that. You are not attracted to people who don't have the same basic standards, so you don't welcome them into your life. You are not desperate to cling to bad relationships because you don't fear being alone. You walk tall in your skin and hold yourself accountable to a high standard.

So, you can see that when you have low self-esteem, it's easy to make poor choices. When your self-esteem is high, you make better, less emotionally charged decisions.

Make no mistake, self-esteem is your biggest driver in every aspect of your life.

## The Importance of Emotional Mastery

Do you ever feel like you can't get control of your thoughts or emotions? Do you suddenly get angry or easily triggered by a negative behavior trait? Do you sometimes think so much that you become physically disabled by your thoughts and you can't continue a task, feeling overwhelmed?

These are all signs of not having emotional mastery. Emotional mastery is when you are in control of your feelings and you have achieved complete emotional control.

Is this a place that is easy to get to? No, not at all; but you can get there if you begin regular self-awareness practices that you continue to add to your life. Emotional mastery is a journey with no set destination, simply a path that evolves, shapes, and grows over time. Emotion mastery leads to emotional intelligence and is one of the most beneficial skills you can acquire in your lifetime.

## Heartfelt Checkpoint 1

One of the features of this interactive workbook is to check in with yourself after each chapter. Before we begin your deep work, it's important to know where you are right now in your journey of self-awareness. Your self-awareness and emotional intelligence are the assets that will carry you through on this path when times get rough and you feel like giving up.

And feeling like giving up is normal on this path of improvement.

Remember, shadow work is the work we leave until last. It's the work we do usually because we have to; it is rare that we willingly walk into this arena. It's the work that if we don't do it, will trip us up and keep us from the work and mission we are meant for.

You are strong.
You are brave.
You can do this.

### *Self-Discovery Milestones*

Answer the following statements honestly, using your heart as a guide to feel into your responses. Remember, there are no right or wrong answers:

**I understand my emotions when they come up, and I'm able to identify why I am feeling them.**

Always
Often
Sometimes

Not often

Never

**I can express my opinion and defend myself.**

Always

Often

Sometimes

Not often

Never

**I do not compare myself with others.**

Always

Often

Sometimes

Not often

Never

**I know my own boundaries.**

Always

Often

Sometimes

Not often

Never

**I set boundaries with others.**

Always

Often

Sometimes

Not often

Never

**I know what's holding me back.**

Always

Often

Sometimes

Not often

Never

**I acknowledge and understand my fears.**

Always

Often

Sometimes

Not often

Never

**I know when I am slipping into negative self-talk.**

Always

Often

Sometimes

Not often

Never

**I have compassion for myself, and I feel self-love.**

Always

Often

Sometimes

Not often

Never

**I can identify my bad habits.**

Always

Often

Sometimes

Not often

Never

**I am working on my bad habits because I know they are not serving me.**

Always
Often
Sometimes
Not often
Never

**I set goals that are good for me and are aligned with my dreams.**

Always
Often
Sometimes
Not often
Never

**I know my strengths and weaknesses, and I steer my actions so I'm working on the things I am good at.**

Always
Often
Sometimes
Not often
Never

**I make intentional decisions that align with my beliefs and value system.**

Always
Often
Sometimes
Not often
Never

**I nurture my relationships, and I explore new ones.**

Always
Often
Sometimes

Not often

Never

**I can forgive myself easily for choices I made in the past when I did not know any better.**

Always

Often

Sometimes

Not often

Never

**I know myself and my worth, and I accept the things I cannot change.**

Always

Often

Sometimes

Not often

Never

**I take steps to work toward my ultimate dream and goals in life.**

Always

Often

Sometimes

Not often

Never

## *Results*

Always: If you scored mostly always, you are on the right track toward complete self-discovery. Well done, you! You've put in the hard work, and you're now reaping the benefits of understanding yourself better and working toward total alignment and fulfillment.

**Often:** If you score mostly often, you are on an enlightened path of self-discovery and you're understanding more about yourself daily.

**Sometimes:** If you scored sometimes, you've started your journey into self-awareness and now you need to practice consistency. Create a routine so you can further your exploration.

**Not Often:** If you scored not often, it's okay. What will help you get on the path to self-discovery is taking the time for self-reflection so you can understand yourself better.

**Never:** If you scored never, then this is the perfect time to start. Don't worry, we all started at the beginning, and this is the introduction to a beautiful, uplifting journey for yourself!

Now that you've firmly accepted where you are in your self-awareness journey, let's move on to deepen your connection to your shadow by understanding what it is and how it's affecting your life.

# Celebration 1

Now that you've completed the very first section of your shadow work workbook, put on your favorite movie or show and relax, congratulating yourself for taking the first step!

# CHAPTER 1
# UNDERSTANDING THE SHADOW SELF

Nobody wants to look at their dark side. We are willing and curious to unpick the dark elements of others' characters; but when it comes to our own, we often view ours with fear and shame.

So, what you're embarking on is brave—extraordinarily brave.

In this section of the workbook, we are going to take a deep look at what exactly is the shadow self. By truly understanding the key to unlocking your limitations, you will be able to take your life to the next level.

The next level of health, wealth, and happiness. Let's get started.

## Defining the Shadow Self

The shadow self is also known as your dark side, the side of you that you are hiding from, have disowned, or repressed. The reason why we have unclaimed pieces of ourselves is that these are very often undesirable character traits. To explain what shadow aspects are, can you identify a time when you have acted out of character? Or is there a relationship where you feel embarrassed by your behavior? Check out the following list and ask yourself if you recognize any of these aspects in your character:

- greed
- jealously
- anger
- selfishness
- power hungry
- desire
- arrogance
- manipulation
- dishonesty
- cruelty
- stubbornness
- impulsivity
- impatience
- indecisiveness
- rudeness
- narcissism
- pessimism
- entitlement
- closemindedness
- egotism
- laziness
- intolerance

It is hard to face up to some of these characteristics, and not all of them are negative. However, the truth is that we all have many of these facets showing up in our personalities, and we don't want others to notice them. They creep in and seep out when we are not being our best selves. We need to mindfully communicate with others and work on increasing our emotional intelligence.

In a nutshell, we actively disown any characteristic that does not align with the way we want to be perceived. This forms your shadow self.

These disowned parts of you sit in your unconscious and usually show up when you're triggered or unable to master your emotions. If we own and acknowledge these pieces of ourselves, they don't interfere too much in our daily lives. However, when we fail to see them, that's when they creep up and cause chaos.

## How the Shadow Self Is Formed

As a human, we come into this world with a whole range of emotions, both good and bad. If we are born with all these traits, you would think we should be able to use all of them, right? But from early childhood, we are punished for displaying negative emotions. For example, if you shouted or got angry with a sibling, were your toys taken away? Or, were you grounded for "talking back," to your mom or dad?

At this time, you were expressing an emotion you were feeling, but societal norms and socialization dictated that it was not good to express these emotions. It's likely you would be punished if you decide to display them. So, you hid them. Your primary caregivers, most likely your mom or dad, would have discouraged you from anger, shouting, crying, or even questioning. You were guided to hide or disown these emotions. And these created the shadow self.

So, for the first part of your life and education in this world, you believed you had a shadow, or a dark side, your bad side—the part of you that was not going to be liked by yourself or others. By hiding these aspects of you, you became unconscious of their presence and when they show up now, you deny them. You refute them. You blame others. You can't get rid of these features of your character, you simply bury and ignore them. This is your shadow self.

To accept this part of yourself—your shadow—you have to begin the process of unlearning everything you've learned so far about emotions.

# The Impact of the Shadow in Your Life

"Unless we do conscious work on it, the shadow is almost always projected; that is it is neatly laid on someone or something else so we do not have to take responsibility for it." –Robert Johnson.

Your shadow will show up like a mirror. The things you dislike in another person are very often hiding in your shadow self. This is a gut-wrenchingly difficult statement to digest, as oftentimes, you will feel so strongly about these personality features that you become triggered and react badly to others who show you these traits.

Let me tell you a story about Melissa. Melissa always prided herself on being calm and patient, letting others speak first and remaining quiet and composed in the face of challenges, especially at work. Melissa had never undertaken any shadow work before.

One day, during a team meeting, one of her colleagues spoke up passionately and confidently about a project Melissa was also involved in. As a result of that, a lively debate took place between coworkers. Melissa instantly felt angry and upset with her colleague for not remaining calm and collected. There was no confrontational situation during the meeting, so Melissa couldn't understand why she had these emotions. She was confused and couldn't pinpoint where her feelings were coming from, especially since this was one of her favorite colleagues to work with.

This was Melissa's shadow self at work. Melissa had suppressed being outspoken and passionate as a child, as her parents favored calm, quiet, "speak when you're spoken to" behavior. Melissa had denied her voice. In this work situation, Melissa's shadow showed up very strongly, as Melissa had denied these aspects of her character. Her anger came from not being able to express herself in the way she needed to. Her anger was also fueled by knowing these are positive personality traits that someone can be rewarded for having, just like her colleague was during the team meeting. This sparked jealousy and resentment in Melissa. In truth, the emotions Melissa was feeling about her colleague were all about herself and her lack of being able to express herself in alignment with who she felt she really was.

In Melissa's case, we can see that the shadow created negative feelings about herself and her colleague. These feelings were hard to resolve and stayed with her in the days ahead. But it didn't end there. This reaction created more problems in feelings of guilt and shame for reacting this way about a friend and not having the courage to do the shadow work to retrieve these pieces of herself. From this one small incident, the shadow not only appeared but grew in size, too.

So, how does your shadow impact your life? Let's look at it in two ways.

## The Negative Impact of Your Shadow Self

Your shadow self, if left hidden and ignored, will trip you up. Imagine it as a secret or a skeleton in your closet. At some point, it will expose you, and your reaction to it will be to run as fast as you can.

Your shadow, untamed, will cause chaos in your life. We gently touched on the negative impact of the shadow self that results in being unable to reach your goals fully or having a life of chaos. Your shadow will subconsciously attract the wrong people and, subsequently, your judgment won't be based on your whole, complete character. You'll make bad decisions and poor choices, and your alignment will be off. You'll struggle to feel fulfilled, perhaps always getting so far up the road and then having to give up. Not accepting your shadow is reflected in an incomplete life and life mission.

The emotional impact of this is usually reactive, impulsive behavior, feeling triggered, and shutting down further parts of yourself to cope with what's happening to you. In addition to that, you might be experiencing feelings of guilt or shame, knowing that you have character traits that you feel are ugly and should not be exposed to others.

If you have toxic behaviors, self-sabotage, or even more advanced mental health concerns—for example, hoarding—these can be part of the negative impact of the shadow self. Not dealing with them causes shame, anxiety, and further negative emotions to increase over time.

## *The Positive Impact of Your Shadow Self*

"Authenticity" has become a bit of a buzzword recently and probably for the wrong reasons. However, it is the word used to describe how your character will become once you've accepted and understood your shadow self.

When you welcome in all the unwanted, undesirable pieces of yourself, your character becomes whole. Your interactions with others are genuine, and you are naturally calmer and mindful. Your emotional intelligence increases, and you sit within your skin comfortably.

You rarely experience the impulse to overreact and create drama, accepting what is and living in the present moment. Owning your shadow is deeply empowering and boosts your confidence, too.

In the process of accepting your entire being, warts and all, your path to fulfillment starts to open up to you. You make better decisions, focus on what you truly want, and set life goals that are aligned with your dreams.

Life is calmer, more peaceful, and more mindful when you take time to enjoy breathing, a sunset or sunrise, and simple moments of pleasure found in the joy of being alive.

And the good news is you've already started walking this path, right here, right now.

Well, that was a lot to take in, and I want you to pause before we assess how your shadow self is showing up in your life right now.

Grab a coffee or your favorite herbal brew, snuggle under a blanket, and relax as we check into your heart space with Heartfelt Checkpoint 2.

# Heartfelt Checkpoint 2

This is your next checkpoint. You must follow up on your shadow work learning with opportunities to explore what is happening for you. Remember that you are on this journey here and now, as this is part of your evolutionary path. Everything is right. Everything is as it should be. Nothing is given to you that you cannot deal with. You have everything inside of you that you need. Your time to explore, rest, and restore is now.

To go back in time to your childhood, I want you to find a quiet corner, where you can light a candle and lie down to gently journey back to your childhood years.

We will go on a pathway to meet your inner child and see what emotions they are feeling.

We will greet them in love and spend a little time with them.

When you're comfortable, your phone is on "Do Not Disturb," and you're ready, let's begin.

## *Guided Meditation: A Visit to Meet Your Inner Child*

Find a comfortable space. Lie down or sit back in your chair if you can. Close your eyes and take a walk with me, back in time.

Breathe deep. Feel your body, each limb heavy and relaxed.

Relax your forehead and your mind, and release the tension in your face, especially around your jaw.

Connect your safety line to the present moment and gently close the door to now.

Let's begin our journey.

Close your eyes.

Take a deep breath in for 6. 1, 2, 3, 4, 5, 6.

And out for 6. 1, 2, 3, 4, 5, 6.

And again, in for 6. 1, 2, 3, 4, 5, 6.

And breathe out for 6. 1, 2, 3, 4, 5, 6.

One last time, breathe in for 6. 1, 2, 3, 4, 5, 6.

And slowly out for 6. 1, 2, 3, 4, 5, 6.

Today, we are on a journey into a timeless dimension to meet your inner child.

This space is free from fear and sadness. It is a space filled with love, compassion, and appreciation for your younger self.

You will meet your inner child today. They may be alone or with others; they may be able to speak; or they will talk to you through sounds and signs. They may not even notice you are there. All settings and scenes are okay. You are safe.

Breathe in again for 6. 1, 2, 3, 4, 5, 6.

And slowly out for 6. 1, 2, 3, 4, 5, 6.

This is a safe place. You and your inner child are protected and loved.

As you slowly take deep breaths in and out, fill your aura with love in a beautiful white light.

Watch as the light grows and grows and fills your aura, from the tip of your crown to the ends of your toes.

Let all that white light and love spill out of your aura and into the space around you.

Your inner child is here. Greet them with love.

Say hello to your inner child. Hold out your arms and let them come to you. Hold them close and fill them with love.

Apologize to your inner child. Tell them you're sorry for not visiting them sooner.

Say "I love you," to your inner child.

Now, what can you feel?

What emotion is your inner child experiencing right now?

Feel into that emotion. You may ask them questions if you want to.

Spend a few moments with your inner child to feel the emotions they are feeling.

What is coming up for them?

Let them talk to you if they can.

Take a few moments to feel deeply into this.

(Pause for two minutes or stop the audiobook and take your time.)

Say to your inner child, "It's okay to feel this emotion. It's okay to feel any emotion." Stay with your inner child while you feel the emotion together; watch it rise like a cloud in the sky, and let the gentle breeze blow it up and away until you can no longer see it.

Hold your inner child and say, "Well done for feeling and releasing that emotion. I'm proud of you. I'll come back soon to spend more time with you."

Tell your inner child you love them and what a good job they've done today.

Say goodbye to your inner child.

Close the door to the world of the past.

Take a moment to transport through time, back to the present.

Back to now. To this very moment.

You arrive at the door now. Open it, walk through it, and release your safety tether.

You are home.

Start to wiggle your fingers and toes.

Slowly open your eyes.

You are back in the present moment. Look around you and ground yourself in the now.

Repeat after me: "I am back in my body, in the present moment. I am complete."

## *Follow Up: Journaling Exercise*

Once your meditation is complete, it's important to record the findings of your inner child meditation for reflection and progress checking. You can do this immediately after your transcendental journey or after a night's sleep. You may need time to process the journey you took with your inner child, and sleep helps us process many thoughts and emotional states.

If any distressing feelings come up during the meditation, remember to always ask for help. Talk to a friend, counselor, or therapist if you need to, especially if it has brought forward an emotion that you cannot release.

Your care and safety are the most important things right now; treat yourself with love and compassion.

If you are ready to continue with the journaling prompts, let's begin.

Take no more than 15 minutes to complete this task, so it remains something you can include in your daily actions and you can stay accountable to your self-awareness work.

Get a journal, specifically for recording your inner child work. Open it up and write down the following five questions about your inner child:

1.  What emotion did your inner child feel today?

2. Why did your inner child feel that emotion?

3. How did that emotion make your inner child feel?

4. What do you wish others understood when you were feeling that emotion?

5. What words did others use to describe you when you were growing up?

Once you have answered all five questions, write down in a few sentences what you would tell your inner child now, so they could feel healed from that experience.

For example, you could write:

"It is okay to feel angry when your toy breaks. It's okay to feel frustration and sadness when something you love is broken. Let that emotion rise up and watch it float by. Do not hold on to that emotion. Feel it and let it pass on by. Everything will be okay."

Remember, if you are holding on to a negative emotion or sadness following your guided meditation, seek help so you can move past it. In the next chapter, we will begin a journey of self-discovery. We will begin your reflection journaling, and I would urge you to start that now, especially if you have some difficult emotions surfacing.

See you in the next section. Remember, I'm with you.

## Celebration 2

But before you continue, it's time to celebrate again. Tonight, should be filled with self-care. Run a warm bath, light a scented candle, and relax, comforting yourself for a job well done!

# CHAPTER 2
# YOUR JOURNEY TO SELF-DISCOVERY

Have you ever been curious about your astrological sign to learn about the facets of your character? Or have you explored numerology to reveal your personality traits? Or maybe you've gone a step further and explored human design to work out how you operate when responding to others? These are all ways we try to discover ourselves and learn what makes us tick. Rather like layers of an onion, there are many ways to access ourselves; and the more we peel back, the more we discover who we truly are, beyond social conditioning and traumatic childhood experiences.

## Assessing Your Current Self-Awareness

In the introduction to the workbook, you took part in a self-discovery assessment.

How did you do? What came up for you?

Today, we're going to take that a little bit further and look at ways you can regularly assess your current self-awareness. You may already be enjoying some of these techniques as part of your journey toward increased emotional intelligence.

## *Journaling*

This technique has to be one of the simplest and most effective ways of assessing your self-awareness because it focuses on reflection. It also provides a diary of how much improvement you've made over time. This becomes an invaluable resource that you can use to measure how far you've come and empower yourself on your journey of self-discovery.

Journaling provides the space for you to be honest and open. It can also help in de-stressing and promoting feelings of improved well-being.

Very often, when you write down a feeling or situation you struggled to deal with, you gain a lot more clarity by expressing the feelings around it in a safe, personal space.

## *Mindfulness Practices*

Mindfulness is simply the art of watching what you say and think, and there are many ways you can do that. Let's take a look at some of these tools, and while we're doing that, imagine the practice in your mind and feel into which ones you'd like to explore:

- **Breath Work:** Self-discovery practices with shadow work can unpick some delicate wounds. First and foremost, it's helpful to have a breathing practice you can fall back on, especially if your thoughts become too overpowering or you've suffered from racing thoughts and overwhelm before.

- **Body Scan:** This is an extremely effective way to see if you're physically holding on to stress related to your shadow. Very often, you can find online guide programs to walk you through body scans to see where you are holding stress. Work through this, adding it to a weekly practice of mindfulness on your self-discovery journey.

- **Shadow Walking:** Developing a process of shadow walking is similar to mindful walking. Set your intention before you begin your walk and decide on pieces of your shadow you want to work on. Think without judgment and pay attention to any thoughts or insights that come up for you.

- **Present Moment Sensory Awareness:** As you journey through pieces of your character, it can be a delicate time filled with thoughts of the past. Introducing present-moment sensory awareness can keep you from falling into old memories and a negative mindset. Focus on eating, bathing, looking around you, and saying what you see, smell, hear, and feel. This will help to keep you grounded, calm, free from distress, and in the present moment.

- **Walking in Nature:** Walking in nature with your shoes off is a very grounding experience, and it doesn't matter where you do it either—local park, forest, or even the beach. Flip off your shoes and ground yourself on the earth, there's nothing quite like it.

- **Mindful Movement Release:** Very often, it is only in the process of physical movement that we uncover parts of ourselves that have been buried deep, as far as our tissues and cells. Practicing movement—dance, sports, working out—can help in the process of bringing emotions to the surface and releasing them naturally into the ether. Set your intention before you begin and get ready to release what comes up.

Any one or all of these practices help you to assess your current self-awareness. If you can begin to create a schedule where you fit one or more of these routines into your daily life, your self-awareness will be constantly evolving.

## Techniques for Uncovering Your Shadow: Journaling Exercises for Self-Discovery

Shadow journaling is one of the most important techniques you will use on this path of self-discovery. But to journal effectively, you need to get to the core of your shadow self. In this section, we will create the questions you need to ask yourself for effective answers that hold the key and get to the heart of your shadow. It's time to unpeel negative feelings you have connected and attached to your emotions.

Take a deep breath and remember that this introspective work will help you become aligned and complete with your true, authentic self. It will be tough, so thank yourself for taking the steps to create a better version of yourself and your life.

Remember that all emotions have positive and negative features, every emotion carries light and shade. There is no need to be fearful of anything that may arise.

If you need to take a pause and prepare your mind for the work that's ahead, then do so. Remember, these questions are wrapped in love and compassion, so you can create a whole, unfragmented version of yourself.

For the next 30 days, pick one of the reflective questions and journal the answers. It doesn't matter if you don't have clarity right now. What does matter is that you are walking the path to aligning yourself with your true character in acceptance and love. Some of these questions may touch a nerve; if so, make a note in your journal. What you are ready to face may hold a valuable key to aspects of your shadow. If not right now, you can come back to these prompts and deal with them when you feel ready.

Open your journal and write down the following questions, leaving yourself plenty of space to journal under them:

1.  What personality, character traits, or strong emotions in other people trigger you? These can be either positive or negative.
2.  Are there any recurring patterns and conflicts in any of the relationships you have with others?
3.  Are there any aspects of your personality or character that you have from others, like your mom or dad?

4.  Remember back to the role models you had as a child, what qualities you admire in them, and how they connect with your shadow.

5.  Consider your feelings connected to authority figures, how do you feel around teachers, bosses, or people in positions of power? How do you connect with them, through respect or rebellion, or does any other emotion come up?

6.  Consider your feelings connected to your parents. Are there any unresolved issues that could be connected to your shadow self?

7.  Have you ever compromised one of your values because of another person? Why did you make this choice at that moment?

8.  Do you find forgiving others hard to do or do you hold a grudge? Are these still affecting you and stopping you from healing?

9.  Do you compare yourself to others? Does this cause envy, inadequacy, or competition that may hint these may also be hidden in your shadow self?

10. What emotions come up when someone criticizes or challenges you?

11. Do you ever wear a mask or take on a role to please or communicate with another person?

12. What emotions do you try and hold back or hide from other people?

13. Do you remember something that happened in your childhood that affected your self-worth (the feeling that you're a valuable and unique person, no matter what)?

14. Do you remember something that happened in your childhood that affected your self-esteem (the range of your happiness that can increase or decrease based on what you do and how you see yourself)?

15. What do you think the biggest problem is in your shadow self?

16. Do you suffer from recurring patterns of behavior or patterns

in relationships, which may indicate your shadow holds these aspects of yourself?

17. Do you modify your behavior daily to fit in with people at work or in another setting?

18. Have you ever had an experience where you felt total resistance to something or someone?

19. Do you ever have a recurring dream or nightmare, and is there anything symbolic about these experiences that you could look into to discover what's hiding in your shadow?

20. Is there anything in your identity—religion, sexual orientation, ethnicity—that you choose to hide and not show others?

21. What self-limiting beliefs do you hold?

22. Have you ever felt like an outsider or that you didn't belong? How did that make you feel?

23. What does your negative self-talk sound like? Give as many examples as possible.

24. How do you cope with stress? What emotions come up and how does this change your behavior?

25. Is there a goal or dream you have not pursued because of feelings of self-doubt?

26. What is your behavior like during an argument, disagreement, or challenge with family or those close to you? How do you show up?

27. Do you have any fantasies about your life that you feel are completely unattainable?

28. What triggered moments of massive personal growth in your life? How can you build on those?

29. What is your version of success, how does it look, and do you expect to achieve it?

30. If you could remove the limitations of your shadow, what would your character be like? What strengths and unique qualities would you have?

## Heartfelt Checkpoint 3

Already you have held yourself accountable by reaching Chapter 2, and you must be feeling a huge sense of relief and determination to continue uncovering your shadow.

Just by being here, you have achieved something remarkable, and I know how much effort and strength this journey takes. You are determined to see this journey to the next level, and your heart must be bursting with pride right now.

To stay on this road takes great courage; courage I know you have. But life has a funny way of throwing us a curveball or two sometimes, and I want to ensure that you walk this journey to the next stop and feel an amazing sense of self and renewed pride.

So, let's begin our accountability schedule to cope with unreleased trauma, past emotions, fear, and negative thinking.

Take out your diary or calendar and mark down an ideal mindfulness schedule. We are consciously not going call it to shadow work because of the negative connotations; this can lead to avoiding doing the work. Most people throw themselves into personal growth without even undertaking shadow work, which leaves them incomplete. You're not going to be one of them.

## *Mindfulness Transformation Schedule*

To make you more comfortable, we will use the umbrella of Mindfulness Transformation Planner.

Ideally, you should have check-in points every day:

- **Morning:** On waking, check in with your mindfulness for the day. You can choose from morning meditation, reflective journaling, priming yourself with breathing exercises and visualization, setting intentions, and positive affirmations. Make sure to acknowledge any feelings and emotions that come up overnight.
- **Midday:** Take a simple five-minute check to acknowledge any thoughts or feelings that have surfaced throughout the

morning.

- **Afternoon:** Work on some of the journaling prompts. Don't go too deep, but continue with at least one question to move you forward on your shadow work journey.
- **Evening Reflection:** Use this opportunity to do reflective journaling about the day and to acknowledge and release any emotions before sleeping.

If you are not ready to embrace this journey fully, perhaps you have a very demanding job or family responsibilities, and that's okay. Do not be hard on yourself. However, the more points you have throughout the day, the faster your transformation will take place.

Make sure that you are accountable to at least one of the daily tasks, and if you can only manage one right now, ensure it is either the morning waking to check in or the evening reflection.

Let's look at how far you've come already. The next piece of the puzzle is self-esteem boosting, and we are going to find a way to immediately build strength and confidence—no matter what you have experienced in life this far. Join me in Chapter 3.

# Celebration 3

Tonight, I want you to read a book for at least 15 minutes, snuggled up in bed or on a cozy chair, nurturing yourself with different thoughts and time out.

# CHAPTER 3
# SELF-ESTEEM BOOSTING STRATEGIES

Do you wake in the early hours with racing thoughts, or do you sleep peacefully, like a baby, for a full 7-8 hours?

How do you sleep?

What's your bedtime routine?

And why am I asking? Because there are so many self-esteem-boosting strategies that make up your daily routine that you can fix right now without adding extra work into your day. So next, let's launch into strategies and exercises to increase your self-esteem naturally and simply. We can identify how you may have lowered it without realizing it, and then we can figure out what you can do it increase it effectively.

I want you to be mindful of the four main pillars that make up your life:

- sleeping
- eating
- spending time outside

- physical activity

Immediately, your brain is going to flag one of these four areas where you have a weakness. Perhaps your diet isn't good; maybe you don't get outdoors every day; maybe you can't sleep well or you've stopped working out.

And I'm sure you've heard it before, but these areas of your life are vital to master for the health of your mind, body, and soul.

Vital.

Each one of these categories shows the measure of self-love that you give to yourself:

- To eat nourishing foods is to treat your body, your temple, with love.
- To rest well is to gift your body and brain the correct amount of time to restore and heal daily.
- To work out is to cherish the body you have, push out all toxins, and build strength to keep your body's mechanisms working to support your life.
- To spend time outside is to gift yourself your home environment; you belong to the trees, the sea, and the wilderness. You will find restorative power here away from electric vibrations and the energies of the city or built-up areas.

Which of the above categories did you feel some resistance around when I mentioned them? Which areas do you feel proud of? Maybe here, it's time to take a moment to pause. If anything came up of you while you were in this section, add it to your journal. These fundamental pillars of life are the aspects that most people find hard to deal with, and we see this everywhere in obesity, health problems, depression and anxiety, and disconnection.

You are not alone.

So now, let's get back to your shadow and see how the shadow uniquely affects self-esteem.

# Recognizing How the Shadow Effects Self-Esteem

Your shadow directly affects your confidence. Let me explain how.

When you hide parts of yourself and deny aspects of your character so you "fit in" or "get on" with people to make you "one of the crowd," your confidence bombs. You can't be yourself fully when you have to watch what you say and do. You show up as an incomplete version of yourself; and while you may be able to do this for a time, you certainly won't be able to sustain it. And eventually, others will also start to notice it.

But when you can show your true face and voice to the world, you show up whole. You are fully integrated and who you are supposed to be. You are who you were born to be, and this version of yourself not only commands confidence but also attaches all that is good and plentiful to your being. This, in turn, creates your path of alignment; your path to fulfillment, and that, in turn, compounds you with more confidence.

Your shadow is vital to your self-esteem. Let's look at how it works.

When you accept parts of yourself you're not happy with, you dislike, or you feel shame about, it becomes easier to bring them into the light. By bringing them into the light, you can manage these aspects of your character better when they surface.

When you haven't accepted your shadow, do you notice any of these behaviors in yourself, where your confidence is directly reduced by your hidden shadow?

- You are happy to say hello and introduce yourself at gatherings but nervous to initiate conversation.
- You think people are judging the way you look or the clothes

you are wearing.

- You think others are better than you or you think they think they are better than you.

- You have mild paranoia and think others are looking at or talking about you.

- You are reluctant to take food from a buffet or self-service area and wait for others to go first.

- You feel awkward for all, or a large part, of the time.

- You regularly second-guess yourself, and you think about your past actions, or what somebody said to you, over and over again.

Conversely, when your shadow is integrated and you are doing shadow work, you may behave differently:

- You are excited to go to social gatherings, even when you don't know anyone there.

- You are comfortable to eat alone in restaurants.

- You can go to the cinema alone.

- You can talk to others and initiate conversations without thinking about it.

- You don't dwell on what you could have said or done differently or over what someone said to you.

Where did you recognize yourself and your actions here? Remember, whatever comes up for you is valuable—add it to your journal, as this is another piece of your journey.

And don't forget to thank yourself for being honest and open about this. Compassion for yourself is the key to helping you continue this work. You've worked on some dark corners of yourself here; make sure you move on immediately to Building Self-Love and Self-Worth.

## Building Self-Love and Self-Worth

What's the difference between self-love and self-worth? The best way to describe self-love is to think about how you treat your friends. Consider the way you want to make them laugh, have fun with them, treat them to gifts or days out, listen to them, spend time with them, and help them; that's exactly how you want to treat yourself. Behaving this way with yourself is self-love.

Now, this self-love builds self-worth. Self-worth is knowing that no matter what, you are amazing and you are valuable. Self-love is the road to self-worth.

## *Self-Love*

Let's begin with self-love.

Pause here and take a moment to think about your typical day. What do you do each day to instill self-love?

Take a moment to think about the following questions:

- Do you write down gratitude statements?
- Do you say private affirmations out loud?
- Do you practice mindfulness to guard your brain against negative thinking?
- Do you pause, rest, and take breaks during your work schedule?
- Do you allow time to eat, away from all distractions?
- Do you do something you like each day, like reading, dancing, drawing, or listening to music? Something that connects you to yourself and lights you up?
- Do you limit time on social media and other screen-time entertainment?
- Do you celebrate your wins, even things as small as checking off your to-do list?
- Do you make time for yourself, instead of thinking "I don't have time"?

If you're not doing any of these, where can you make a start today?

What small practice can you add immediately to your schedule? If you're finding yourself thinking, "I don't have time to do this," this resistance could be coming from your shadow self. Remember to jot this down in your journal, so you can explore what not making time for yourself means. For example, if you're so busy, does this stop you from thinking about other things in your life? Is being so busy and having no time simply a distraction from something you're avoiding?

Take another pause to clear your head. Notice what thoughts are coming up for you now, both the positive and the negative. It's in these moments that you will gain complete clarity, these moments when you are alone and can be completely honest with yourself. These moments are your lightbulb moments. These moments will move you forward.

So, think about your day and implement at least one practice to move the needle. Make sure you do it in bite-sized chunks, otherwise, you won't implement it and stick to it. Small, incremental practices are much easier to turn into habits.

## *Self-Worth*

Now it's time to move on to self-worth. Increased self-esteem has a very different feeling from increased self-love. Self-worth is tied to your confidence and self-belief. You can have a strong sense of self-worth even if your self-love feels lower. For example, you can have undeniable self-beliefs even if you don't like yourself too much. But what increased self-love does is create an even stronger sense of self-worth.

Building self-worth works a slightly different way. Self-worth can emphasize personal attributes. Let's go through each one to fully understand how they connect to self-worth:

1. **Achievements:** This refers to your success and achievement. Things that you've done, and that could be anything where you have felt personal accomplishments, breakthroughs, triumphs, gains, or milestones.
2. **Recognition:** This centers on others' awareness of your

abilities, being acknowledged for your skills, or being awarded for your efforts and contribution.

3. **Self-Respect:** The boundaries you set play a huge role in establishing and maintaining self-respect, and this also includes how you treat yourself generally.

4. **Inner Strength:** This touches on your mental strength, the way you deal with upset, and challenges when you're faced with adverse conditions.

5. **Faith:** Your faith is the belief in something you cannot see; this could be your higher self, religion, or spirituality and is usually at the core of your driving force.

Take a moment to pause here and think about your achievements, recognition, self-respect, inner strength, and faith. Do you feel that any one of these areas is lacking? Do you feel any resistance to these personal attributes? Remember to journal any feelings that are surfacing and pay attention to where you feel them in your body. This will also provide you with key insights into how your shadow is playing a part in your self-worth.

You've taken a lot in on self-esteem and self-worth, so before we leave this chapter, let's create affirmations that you can use immediately to reinforce positive language and emotions about yourself.

## Affirmations and Self-Esteem Exercises

The next stop on your journey is to make authentic affirmations. Affirmations, when used with other self-esteem exercises, can significantly boost your self-worth.

Choose five of the following self-love affirmations, then choose five of the self-worth affirmations to make your own authentic list of confidence boosters. Remember, these strategies work better when they mean something to you, so if you can create more personal ones, they will have greater significance and work much faster:

### *Self-Love Affirmations*

1. I love and accept myself fully.
2. I love myself just as I am today.
3. I love every part of my life, and I am grateful for each moment.
4. I am my own best friend, and it is natural to love myself.
5. I deserve a life filled with love and happiness.
6. I love being with myself, and I am kind to myself.
7. I choose to feel joy above any other emotion.
8. Great things happen to me.
9. I am in control and stand in my power.
10. I am beautiful inside and out.

### *Self-Worth Affirmations*

1. I show up for myself every day in the best way possible.
2. I am confident and love myself and my body.
3. I am capable of achieving all my goals and dreams.
4. I forgive myself for making decisions when I did not know any better, and I trust all the decisions I make.
5. I am capable of achieving anything I want to.
6. I deserve love and respect from others.
7. I am enough, and I have always been.
8. I feel calm and peaceful and can handle any challenge that comes my way.
9. I praise myself and others all the time.
10. I redirect negative experiences into powerful opportunities for growth.

Now that you've created your own list of affirmations, let's put that into action with your next Heartfelt Checkpoint. Affirmations work well when combined with other practices, so let's jump into journaling prompts to help you firmly instill these self-empowering beliefs.

## Heartfelt Checkpoint 2

In your next checkpoint, I want you to think back to Chapter 2 where we discussed checking in with yourself during different parts of the day. Now that you know how much your daily routine can affect your mindfulness, here are a variety of journaling prompts you can use to keep you on track, boosting self-esteem while working through your shadow work.

Pause before you begin this work and take time to set your intention, which will enable you to answer more honestly and in alignment with your goals.

## *Daily Routine Journaling Prompts*

- What small change can I make to each of my meals to make them healthier?
- What can I eat less of?
- What can I eat more of?
- How can I get outdoors each day for at least 20 minutes?
- Where can I feel nature's strength, peace, and calm to help me feel good?
- Where can I include this in my day that doesn't cause me to feel stress?
- How can I include exercise in my day?
- How do I love to move my body?
- Where can I incorporate this in my day so I don't feel stressed and look forward to doing it?
- What bedtime routine can I create so I am fully rested and restored?
- How can I create a routine where I fall asleep naturally when the sun goes down and then wake naturally when the sun rises?

Pause again before moving on. Sometimes, when we go deep into our unconscious or belief system, we don't treat ourselves with enough compassion. Rest a little, unwind, take a bath or warm shower, light a candle, and take some deep breaths. Take out your journal, begin on your self-love journaling prompts, and finish with self-love affirmations up next.

## *Self-Love Journaling Prompts*

1. Identify an underlying belief about yourself. Where does this come from? When was the first time you noticed this belief? Do you think it is stopping your healing process?
2. List the things you still have not forgiven yourself for. Why have you not forgiven yourself yet?
3. List the qualities the best version of yourself would hold.
4. Why do you think you struggle to love yourself? What is holding you back?
5. What is your biggest insecurity? How can you learn to love that?

Before moving on to self-worth journaling prompts, take a moment to pause again, make sure you won't be distracted, and have the time to answer openly and thoughtfully. Note that each time you do this exercise different things may come up, and that's okay.

Always close any hard work practice with self-worth affirmations so you can feel strong and empowered.

## *Self-Worth Journaling Prompts*

1. What have I achieved that makes me feel proud of myself?
2. What comes up when I compare myself to others? How can improve this quality so I feel better about myself?
3. Did you feel unloved as a child? What can you do now to repair those feelings?
4. What is a consistent negative thing I tell myself? How can I change the wording to make this an empowering statement instead?
5. What is the one thing I love and appreciate in myself that does not come from any external source or validation?

Use these journaling prompts at your check-in points as part of your daily shadow work practice or create your own if you can develop more meaningful ones. Once you've finished your journaling prompts, remember to always close them with self-esteem-boosting affirmations. This way, while you've dived deep into personal areas of sensitivity, you close your mind with empowering, uplifting phrases of love and compassion for yourself.

## Celebration 4

Today's celebration is to take all that love you've boosted in yourself and share it with a friend. Go for an empathy walk and talk and listen to a friend for at least 30 minutes. Let them share their issues with you, without you talking about yourself at all. Practice active listening; this is a beautiful gift to share now that you are creating an increased sense of emotional intelligence.

## CHAPTER 4
# EMOTIONAL MASTERY

Emotional mastery is not something you have; it's something you do. Nor is it a destination; it's a practice. Being able to manage your emotions, regulate them, appreciate that they are subjective, and understand everybody's interpretation of emotions can be different. It's the process of communicating effectively using the right emotion, and it's a practice that we all need to consistently work on.

## Exploring Emotional Intelligence

Emotional intelligence is understanding your emotions and using them appropriately, and in the process, helping others do the same. It is an ongoing commitment you undertake to repeatedly produce a better version of yourself. Emotional intelligence will get you further than any level of qualification you hold, simply because you will have less destructive behavior in your life.

Emotional intelligence guides us to make better decisions and choices for ourselves. If we can look at situations with a calm, peaceful perspective, we are often better equipped to fine-tune our selection process and avoid chaos, drama, and self-sabotage. Emotionally charged or reactive choices often include all three of those.

Think back to a time when you made an emotionally fueled decision. What happened?

Let's take the example of Jess. After a heated discussion with her boss, Jess quit her job in a rage. She was solely responsible for the finances in her home, and as a consequence of her actions, her family sank into debt, and all family communication became strained. Her husband felt particularly pressured, and their relationship suffered.

Now, if Jess had been emotionally intelligent, what do you think she would have done?

Perhaps take a step back to gather her thoughts? Maybe she could have explained to her boss that the disagreement left her feeling unsure and she'd like time to respond. Both these actions are perfectly reasonable; and Jess, once she had calmed down, would have had the ability to talk things through with her superior in a much calmer way.

Now, in your journal, think of the last time you made an emotionally loaded decision and write it down. What emotions did you feel when this situation happened? Were these emotions directly related to the problem or were they connected to something else? What would you have done differently if you had not felt these emotions?

Pop the kettle on, and don't judge yourself, simply answer the questions without shame, guilt, embarrassment, or regret. Know that this is the first step to improving future choices for yourself and forgive yourself for not being the best version of yourself at that time.

## Understanding and Processing Repressed Emotions

Understanding what a repressed emotion is can sometimes feel baffling. Especially since people who repress emotions tend to be forgetful. This type of emotion is one that's been pushed to one side. It's not been allowed to come out into the open and be felt. And that's okay for some of the time, especially if you are in a situation where your emotions can cause problems for you, such as in the workplace. However, in the long run, if the emotion stays shut down and cut off, it's going to come back to haunt you. Oftentimes, when you least expect it and at the drop of a hat!

This is why we sometimes see people explode.

A lot of repressed emotions have their roots deeply anchored in a childhood experience of trauma. That can mean that that emotion has been pushed down for a long, long time.

Have you ever watched a movie with an emotional scene that made you ball your eyes out immediately? It's like you are connected with the emotions in that part of the movie; the connection hits you deeply, and the movie acts as a floodgate, opening up your emotions with a very intense reaction.

But really the question is, how do I know if I have repressed emotions? Well, there are a few questions you can ask:

- Do I frequently feel numbness or emptiness?
- Do I often and without reason feel anxiety, sadness, or stress?
- Do I feel uneasy or uncomfortable when others start talking about their emotions?
- Do I maintain a cheerful and calm presence to avoid feeling anything else?
- Do I get annoyed when someone asks me how I'm feeling or enquires about my emotions?

The repression of your emotions probably happened most when you were a child, and you would have acted swiftly, as you may have been punished by your parents for expressing certain emotions. You may have been told to "buck up" when feeling disappointed or been scolded for being angry when you were filled with rage. Rather than your primary caregiver explaining what was happening and why you were feeling that emotion, you were instructed to cut it off. You may have even told yourself to shut down and deal with your feelings at a later point. Compartmentalization can happen as a consequence of this and, of course, this also makes up part of your shadow.

The question now is, how do you go about accessing those parts of you that are closed off or buried so deep, that you don't even know what's in there?

# Techniques for Managing and Mastering Your Emotions

First of all, it's important to understand that managing and mastering your emotions is an endless exploration of the self. Some techniques will work well for you, others may not, and that will also change over time.

It's also a good idea to try different techniques. You may not vibe with some of them now, but as this journey takes you into different emotional states, your needs will also change and your practices will develop, too.

Let's look at the different techniques and ways to manage and master your emotions:

### *Naming Your Emotions*

This is the process of saying out loud "I am feeling sad," or "I am feeling angry" when this feeling rises within you. This is the first step in becoming emotionally aware, and it's something that many people avoid. There is calm and clarity in being able to say how you're feeling and ask yourself, Is this emotion relevant right now or is it connected to something deeper? Either way, you'll get an answer that enables you to move past the feeling and get clarity on your thoughts.

### *Emotion Observation*

This technique focuses on watching your emotions rise and float away like clouds once you've acknowledged the feeling. It's a mindfulness practice that's helpful to do in a quiet space, similar to meditation, or you can do it with a guided meditation. Allow yourself to feel into the emotion, visualize it rising into the sky, then floating away in the breeze. This a very helpful technique that pushes you toward increasing your emotional intelligence.

## Deep Breathing

Deep breathing calms the nerves and your body and helps to regulate your nervous system. When you experience an emotion, slowly breathe into it and try not to let it overcome you. Do this as many times as you need to be able to think clearly.

## Body Scans

Body scans are perfect for identifying where you may be holding stress in your body. You can use a guided meditation—there are many free ones found easily online—or try the one below that we will use in our interactive Heartfelt Checkpoint 5. The benefit of a regular body scan is bringing awareness to how your emotions affect your physical body, bringing back your mind swiftly to the present.

## Journaling

As we've touched on before, journaling is possibly the most beneficial of all the shadow work practices. There is something that connects your soul to your mind when you put pen to paper. There are other methods too; speaking out loud and voice memoing your journal can be full of release. You also have the option of online apps and programs to journal in. Journaling is so powerful because it holds a record of reflection, a history of how far you've come, and that's hard to record anywhere else.

## Empathy Walks and Talks

Have you ever taken an empathy walk with another person and just listened to what they say? Have you been able to put yourself aside for 30 minutes or an hour and pay attention to someone else's thoughts or problems? In this space, you can offer your thoughts and perspectives on an issue and help someone else see things from a different point of view. This is an extremely cathartic experience and allows you the peace of mind to put yourself aside for a while.

### *Conflict Resolution*

Asking for help when you need to resolve difficulties is a constructive way to move forward if you have conflicts in relationships, especially personal ones. You can learn effective communication practices, problem-solving methods, negotiating, mediation, how to avoid conflict, and how to draw up a resolution agreement. The scope of conflict resolution goes far and wide, and they are all helpful ways to master your emotions and push you toward greater emotional intelligence.

### *Emotion Regulation Techniques*

Think of emotion regulation techniques as you would for a small child. What comforted you then and what comforts you now? I know for me, a hot bath, essential oils, and a lit candle are all soothers and stabilizers of my emotions. What is personal and works for you? How can you distract or soothe yourself in or after a challenging situation?

### *Positive Coping Strategies*

What makes you laugh? What makes you smile? What makes you light up inside? Think of activities, such as listening to music, dancing, or going to the gym, that you can add to your schedule to avoid negative coping habits, such as drinking alcohol, substance abuse, or overeating.

### *Therapy, Counselling, or Seeking Help*

Last but not least, don't forget how important it is to seek help if you need it. Continued support can be very effective if you are struggling to move past emotions.

## Heartfelt Checkpoint 5

It's your fifth point to check in with yourself, and this time we're going to take the focus away from your mind.

### *Shadow Body Scan*

Put on some restful music that makes you feel calm and at peace and listen to the following body scan guided meditation to watch and observe feelings in your physical being.

In this body scan, we are going to fill your heart with an intention and move that around the body. Light a candle, lean back, or lie down so your body is supported, allowing you to feel every corner of your physical being.

Let's begin.

Take a few deep breaths in and slowly let the air flow out of you.

Breathe deep into your stomach again, allowing the air to blow up your stomach like a balloon, and breathe out.

While you're breathing slowly in and out, think about your intention.

Let's set an intention for today. It can be anything you want, but let's set one before we start.

Notice how your body is feeling right now. Acknowledge it and accept it. Whatever feeling it is, it is perfect for now.

Everything is right and as it should be.

Notice as I'm saying these words if your body is distracted at all or moving you away from your thoughts. Don't judge it, simply notice and acknowledge it.

If you could choose any feeling today, what would it be?

Take a few minutes to decide.

Own that feeling, claim it, and decide to feel that feeling today.

Notice again if any part of your body is distracted, pulling away, or feeling resistance.

Everything is right and as it should be.

Take a few deep breaths in and out.

Welcome all the feelings in your body—peace, resistance—all feelings are welcome. Notice where you feel these feelings in your physical body.

Welcome everything in, even if it is numbness or nothing.

Now, focus your attention on your forehead and feel your intention spreading across or shooting out of your forehead.

Feel as that intention drifts from your forehead down your face into your jaw area and throat.

Is your body resisting or relaxing now?

Is the feeling spreading or can you only manage to spread it in drops?

What feelings are coming up for you?

Let's try again and move that intention from your forehead, jaw, and throat down toward your heart. Can you feel it fill your heart space?

Ask and invite your body to feel your intention; don't force it.

Feel your intention in your heart, filling it with love and beautiful white light flowing from your forehead to your throat and down to your heart.

Now, take a few deep breaths.

We're going to move that glorious white light into your stomach, your emotional center, the place where you store all pain and worry.

Your power is created here. Fill it with beautiful yellow light to empower your gut instincts, your decision-making center. Fill it with sunshine light that radiates directly from your stomach.

Observe any feelings you have in your body. Don't judge. Welcome them all; watch and observe.

Take a few deep breaths and repeat.

Fill your stomach with beautiful yellow light to empower your gut instincts, your decision-making center, and fill it with sunshine light that radiates directly from your stomach.

Breathe deeply into the light.

Now move that beautiful yellow light down your body to a warm orange light, and move it into your sacral area, lower abdomen, and intimate anatomy.

This is your area of creativity, passion, and play. Fill it with warm orange light, letting that intention spill into this area and flow gently further down your body.

Welcome all feelings without judgment; simply watch and observe.

Take a few deep breaths.

Repeat again.

Move that beautiful yellow light down your body to a warm orange light, and move it into your sacral area, lower abdomen, and intimate anatomy. Your place of passion, creativity, and play.

Your passion for life!

Now, we are going to change the warm orange light to a deep red light and connect it to our base, your root, and feel it in the base of your spine and the backs of your legs.

Feel it in your connection with the ground, anchoring you; feel the earth under your feet, supporting you.

Watch and observe how our body feels when we move this invention to your roots, with no judgment, just peace.

Take a few deep breaths.

Repeat again.

Feel the warm, deep red light and connect it to our base, your root, and feel it in the base of your spine and the backs of your legs.

Feel your deep connection with the earth, your spirit lifted with your feet anchored safely in the ground.

Feel the energy of the earth fill your body with support and love and ground your energy into the earth, anchoring this feeling you chose today.

Remember feelings are a choice; you get to choose every single day.

Take a few deep breaths in and out.

And in love and light, connect yourself with the space you are in. Listen to the sounds of the room and the smells; wiggle your fingers and toes and slowly open your eyes.

You are one with your intention. You are complete.

You will feel a deep sense of relaxation in your body following the body scan. Thank your body for letting you into the untold stories and emotions it holds and allow grace to flow in for a body that supports and nourishes you on this journey.

## Celebration 5

Today, a slice of your favorite cake or specialty coffee is on the list of rewards. Your body has done well, and you deserve a little treat for all that hard work!

# CHAPTER 5
# THE SHADOW WORK PROCESS

Working in the unconscious can be a scary concept, and that's where you're going when you work on your shadow. Many practices of psychology, therapy, and even spirituality promote the benefits of shadow work. However, few welcome it in because it is not perceived as the uplifting side of personal growth and healing. Even fewer stick to it. But without practicing shadow work, you will rarely reach the complete version of yourself, as this work is fundamental to finding wholeness within yourself.

Is there a process? Yes, but that process can be different for everyone. In the section of the workbook, we will go through a step-by-step guide to shadow work to get you underway. Let's begin our walk into the shadows.

## Step-By-Step Guide to Shadow Work

The process of uncovering parts of yourself that you have hidden through shame or trauma is never going to be an easy one. However, at this stage, you have learned many self-care tips and practices that will lift you on this journey; and I recommend practicing those even if this journey is lighter than expected. This will lead to greater self-discovery and ultimately increased emotional intelligence, no matter how your passage unfolds.

Any one of the following practices can be used in any order. I will provide you with a step-by-step guide that you can follow; however, during this process, if you change direction and feel that some of the practices mentioned further down the list would help you sooner, feel free to deviate and explore what works for you.

The final process of integration is very important to move past old triggers and hidden behaviors. Integration of the denied pieces of yourself reduces your shadow. Your shadow becomes filled with light and dissipates, and this is your end goal.

## Step 1: Set Your Intention

Before undertaking any self-care practice, it helps to set your intention. An example of this might be, "I no longer want to feel anger when someone is rude to me" or "I want to heal my relationship with my mother." This will help you to stay on track and keep you guided when delving into different emotions that have brought about negative feelings and experiences.

## Step 2: Feel Into the Feeling

Try to feel the emotion or the feeling the emotion generated if you can. If it's hard to get there, go back to a place in your mind where you first felt that feeling. If that's impossible, go to the next step of identifying triggers.

## Step 3: Identify Triggers

This is a slightly different way to tackle shadow work and get to buried emotions, especially if they came about due to trauma. Try reverse engineering to get to the core of the repressed emotion. Think about your triggers, dealing with just one at a time. Tap into the last time you were triggered. What feeling arose? Was it relevant in that moment or tied to an experience? If it was an experience, what words pop into your mind? For example, Jane was abandoned by her mother at an early age, creating feelings of being not important. Jane is triggered when someone is very rude to her, and she reacts badly and often aggressively. This is not because of the rudeness of the other person, who she cares little about. It is because the rudeness makes her feel unimportant, and this feeling connects back to her childhood.

## Step 4: Mediate to Find When You First Felt the Emotion

Now that you've found the origin of the feeling, either from memory or trigger work, try to go back and recall when you first felt that emotion. You want to get a clear picture in your mind of its origin. This will help you accept this feeling and forgive yourself for not managing it better sooner. Thank you past self for sharing it now and helping you to resolve it.

## Step 5: Name the Feeling

Give this feeling a name. This is the fastest way to make this emotion disappear. And you know what? By doing this, you take all the power away from that emotion. Once you recognize it when it surfaces, it's so much easier to handle, and you'll watch yourself become less reactive.

## Step 6: Emotions Leave Feelings in the Body

One of the reasons why you have to do shadow work is because emotions and experiences don't leave thoughts in the body. They leave feelings, codes, signs, and symbols. For example, ill health, shyness or awkwardness, lack of confidence, depression, anxiety, and many, many more. None of these are thoughts; they are symptoms of this experience. This is especially important to recognize and practice regular body scans to fight this issue head-on.

## Step 7: Inner Child Meeting

This can be very difficult for some, and don't expect to meet your inner child straight away. Don't put pressure on yourself to have a conversation with your inner child either. Sometimes, we expect way too much of ourselves, especially if our childhood has been filled with trauma after trauma. You are not alone. Inner child work can take a lot of time. Initially, your inner child may still not want to be found or communicated with; whatever happens, be patient and fill this space with as much love and forgiveness toward yourself as possible. When you get to meet your inner child, ask them questions. For example, what emotion are you feeling today? Or mention an experience to your inner child and ask them to describe how they felt at that time. Remember, patience is key; this part of shadow work is hugely impactful and life-changing.

## Step 8: Journaling

Have you ever looked at an old photo of yourself and noticed how much you've changed? The impact of it is quite incredible; sometimes, those old photos take your breath away! And it's the same with journaling. Flipping back through an old journal, even two or three months previously, it's amazing to see how much your thinking and thought patterns change. For this reason, it's important to document your work. There is also something deeply satisfying in writing your feelings down; by making them real, giving them life, and allowing them to breathe, you can identify their strengths. Where negative feelings are concerned, as soon as they are written down, they lose their power and dissipate fairly quickly.

## Step 9: Recurring Patterns

Another deeply effective way of getting your shadow work underway is looking at recurring patterns in your life. For example, do you always choose the same type of partner—maybe you get stuck in recurring abusive relationships. Or perhaps you always end up chasing a love interest and they repeatedly ghost you. Maybe when things are going well in your life, you blow them up and destroy everything before you reach your goal. These are all signs of recurring patterns of behavior and signs that shadow work needs to be done! Journal on the patterns you see in both your life and behavior and observe how you change these over time.

### *Step 10: Reframe Inner Dialogue*

Once you've started this journey, you can now begin to understand the triggers better and how you'd like to reframe them. Think of changing every "can't" into "can"—reframing is the same kind of process. For example, when you think, I'm overweight and ugly, flip the thought to I love myself just the way I am and feel good about working on the areas of myself I want to improve. Make the reframing of the thought realistic and you'll believe and be guided by these re-routing statements.

### *Step 11: Affirmations and Acceptance*

At this next stage, you've undertaken a lot of heavy emotional work, and that takes its toll on you. That's why affirmations serve you well; they bring you into the present moment, connecting and grounding you, and reinforce believable, compassionate, and empowering statements of improved self-worth. These should be repeated throughout the day, so pin them somewhere you can see them regularly and read or say them out loud as many times a day as possible. These move your thinking into a different version of yourself and are extremely effective. Affirmations bring you toward greater self-acceptance and a more positive self-image.

### *Step 12: Integration*

This is the final step in the shadow work practice. Integration is fundamental to breaking the chains of unwanted behavior and moving you into alignment with who you are supposed to be and your purpose in this life. You take back the missing pieces of yourself, becoming whole and complete. This stops the shadow emitting frequency that attracts more negative things; better things start happening in your life.

Are you still stuck wondering why some people get everything they want and attain abundance? They integrated their shadow work!

## Practical Exercises for Confronting Your Shadow

The first question is, should I confront my shadow or embrace it?

Embracing your shadow is exactly how you approach your shadow work, and I'll show you tips on how to embrace it to bring it out into the open.

Remember, confronting your shadow will make it bigger. You want to bring light to your shadow so you can reduce it and ultimately integrate those lost or discarded pieces of yourself.

The best way to access your shadow is to journal on the following three questions (What is Shadow Work? 2020). These questions will tap into your shadow immediately and bring force to the system. However, when answering these questions, you must do so without judgment, as criticizing them—criticizing yourself—will increase the size of your shadow. Be mindful of this!

Write down the questions and answers to the following questions in your shadow work journal:

1.   What parts of myself do I dislike?
2.   What parts of myself do I judge?
3.   What parts of myself do I fear?

If you want to go a little deeper and include your inner child work—where most of your shadow will have been created—respond to the next set of questions:

1.   Was I completely accepted as a child?
2.   What was expected of me as a child?
3.   What behaviors and emotions were judged by my parents when I was a child?

Lastly, an interesting question that arises from the spiritual side of shadow work may help you to shift some beliefs. I want to include it, as it has an important impact on where you are headed in your life.

● If I wasn't afraid, what would I do with my life?

This last question can be tricky and leave you feeling a little lost, as it's such a big life question. The best way to tackle it is to try some guided visualization exercises to help you see the things you are good at and what you bring to the world.

## Tips for Staying Committed to the Process

Having the staying power to continue ongoing shadow work is a skill in itself. Don't forget, you are extremely brave and one of the few who remain committed to this work! The key to staying on track is to remember why you began shadow work in the first place, and that could have been for many reasons, such as:

- repeated abusive, toxic relationships
- self-destruction and self-sabotage
- failure in manifesting abundance or simply not being able to reach your goals
- healing from unresolved trauma
- self-discovery to increase emotional intelligence

Take out your journal and write down your "why." What brought you to shadow work? What triggers kept coming up that drew you to shadow work in the first place?

Once you fully understand this, it will be much easier to stay committed to the process.

Another way to keep skin in the game is to create your shadow work journals from day one, so you can keep a record of how far you've come and celebrate all your wins. This is a journey you have to actively fill with love and compassion, so go out for dinner, buy that outfit, take a friend for coffee, or treat yourself. Whatever it is, celebrate it! These will become milestones in your journey, and celebration is a pure act of love.

Always stay focused on your transition when doing shadow work. Keep your eye on the end goal. Imagine the new improved version of yourself and visualize it in your mind every chance you get. During visualization, imagine yourself achieving success and feel this and the emotions you'd experience when celebrating. Imagine the celebration of achieving your goal, having the relationship of your dreams, working in your dream job, and living life on your terms. Attach the emotion to your visualization and feel it. Your mind will want to replicate that feeling as fast as possible and will help you get there without you even realizing it.

## Heartfelt Checkpoint 6

It's important to balance shadow work with goals and dreams. And this is the best way to stay committed to the process of shadow work. You have to be working toward something more than just a better version of yourself. You need to see a goal or a vision of how your life might look in three years.

So, in this heartfelt checkpoint, we're going to do a visualization that tells us exactly where you want to be in three years. What's changed since you started doing your shadow work? What dream or goal do you have for yourself? In this visualization, we'll find out, so I want you to light a candle. Sit back in your chair where your body can get nice and heavy or lie down. Make sure the door is closed so you won't be disturbed. And let's begin.

### *Three Years Future Visualization*

Close your eyes and take a few deep breaths in and out, nice and slow.

Let all your limbs relax.

Feel your legs and feet getting heavy.

Feel them firmly on the floor. Feel your buttocks in your chair.

Your back pressed against the back of the chair or on your bed, your arms, and shoulders heavy; your fingers just weightless.

Take a few deep breaths in and out again.

Make sure your eyes are closed and you're in a place of stillness a place of safety.

It's three years in the future.

Imagine you're just waking up; you haven't opened your eyes yet.

You're just lying there, warm and safe.

What can you smell in the room around you?

What can you sense?

What can you hear?

Can you hear cars on a road nearby? Or maybe you can hear birds tweeting outside?

Can you hear water from the ocean or a river?

Or is it complete silence and you're in the mountains?

Feel your arms and your legs; your body feels heavy.

And I want you to slowly open your eyes. What colors can you see?

What can you smell?

What can you hear now?

Pause for a moment.

Think about the sounds and sensations. Now, I want you to sit up slowly.

Put your feet on the floor and slowly look around you.

What can you see? Is there a bed? Maybe a wardrobe, a chest of drawers, and a mirror?

Maybe there's nothing, and your room is empty. What can you see around you?

What colors are the walls? Is there a window? Maybe a balcony? Are you upstairs? Are you downstairs? Where are you?

Take a few deep breaths in and out and completely relax.

Now you're going to walk to the bathroom.

Clean your teeth, wash your face, and feel fresh.

You're slowly going to make your way to the kitchen.

How do you get there? Is it a long hallway? Is it next door? Is it upstairs? Do you walk downstairs? How do you get to your kitchen?

Before you open the door of the kitchen, what can you smell? What can you hear? Is silence in your home or is it laughter?

Do you hear other people? Maybe an animal, a dog barking, a cat meowing?

What do you hear as you open the door? What can you see inside your kitchen?

What colors are here? Who is here? What can you smell?

Is someone making you breakfast? Is bacon sizzling, bread baking, or coffee brewing?

Take a few moments to pause and understand who is here. Or are you alone?

Take a mental note of the colors; take note of anything significant that stands out for you.

As you make your favorite drink, make your way back to your bedroom.

Think about putting on your clothes for the day.

What clothes are you putting on? Maybe an outfit for the gym or to work out. Maybe a dance class.

Maybe your business suit. Maybe you're going to speak on a stage.

Are you putting on comfortable clothes and going to your living room to relax and wake up and read a book?

What clothes are you putting on?

What kind of day are you having?

What kind of day is ahead of you?

How do you start your day?

Take a few moments to think about it.

Now, we are slowly going to come back to the present moment. Start to wiggle your fingers and toes; feel your limbs and slowly open your eyes.

You are back in the now.

How do you feel?

And this is where visualization ends.

This visualization should give you enough clarity on what kind of day you desire. Make notes of all the things that you noticed in the visualization and see if they are connected to a current dream or goal you have in mind. Journal about everything that stood out to you in your visualization: colors, people, sounds, where your home is located, its surroundings, what clothes you wore, and where you were heading that day. This gives you significant insight into where you want to be in three years.

A very good way to see a glimpse into the future you desire!

## Celebration 6

Congratulations! You stepped into the future version of yourself. Today, to mark this significant goal, buy something that reminds you of this future self. Did you see a cup in the kitchen, can you go and buy that cup or one similar to create the connection between you and your future self? Were you wearing a particular item of clothing? Can you buy an item similar to that, again, to remind you of the future and hold that vision alive?

# CHAPTER 6

# HEALING AND INTEGRATION

We've touched on the best orthodox ways to heal your shadow throughout this book. All of these practices take time and are the most effective if they are practiced regularly. However, both healing and integration have some unorthodox practices you may have already heard about and find helpful to explore.

## Alternative Methods for Healing and Transforming Your Shadow

During the process of healing, your shadow will begin to transform; it will reduce in size and power. Different people find different ways of successfully reducing their shadow from many practices, including alternative ones. Some of those could be useful to you, too. Let's check them out.

### *Past-Life Regression*

There are two perspectives on shadow work. The first, held by psychologists, is that your shadow is created in your childhood. The second perspective, held by the spiritual community, is that your shadow is created in all of your lifetimes, in any dimension. What this could mean is if you are aware of a piece of your shadow that you find impossible to connect to any experience, perhaps it was created previously in a past life. Past life regression may hold the key to helping you explore that.

The process of past life regression is very simple. It involves using meditation or hypnotherapy as a tool to go back through time to find untapped memories and experiences. In that space, there may be a piece of your shadow, created from an experience that your conscious self cannot access.

The practice itself can be done through guided meditation or with a practitioner; if you choose to work with someone personally, make sure you get a good recommendation beforehand.

## Akashic Records and Shamanic Journeying

Another way to connect with your shadow is by using Akashic records. These records refer to a place thought of as the library of thoughts from the past, present, and future, which can be accessed by anyone, or any other life form, in this dimension or the multi-dimension. Using a meditation process, it's very easy to get there, and your experience in the Akashic records can be facilitated by a guide.

Again, you can do this practice alone or with a practitioner. This is often helpful, as they will guide you through your visualization and help you ask the right questions while inside the records to retrieve aspects of your character you may have lost or denied. They are also useful in helping you feel complete, which means that you've integrated this discarded piece of yourself successfully before you leave the meditation space.

Shamanic journeying can also take you into your Akashic records with the shaman as your guide, usually using distinctive drumbeats or specific musical sounds.

## Artistic Expression

A beautiful way of accessing your shadow and expressing it

positively is through artistic expression. That can be dance, art, music, writing, or anything that has artistic release. In this way, you'll find a way to let go that lights you up inside and helps you to become a next-level version of yourself. The more you shine brighter by doing the things you love, the smaller and smaller your shadow will become, and this process will help you love yourself and all that's inside your shadow.

## Holotropic Breathwork

This practice can help you access parts of your unconscious by using different breathing patterns. While it's recommended by many, it is beneficial and safer to work with a practitioner who can guide you as you try to tap into higher states of consciousness. The effects of breathwork are said to be deeply healing, but be mindful of any breathwork practice, as you can feel side effects, including nausea and dizziness.

## Sound Healing

Many forms of sound therapy help with shadow work, such as sound baths, singing bowls, shamanic beats, and more. What these sound experiences do, similar to listening to any song you love, is allow you to release emotion. Sound has an energetic level that can help you heal and restore energy in the body, while at the same time releasing tension.

## Family Constellations

This kind of therapy looks at the family dynamic, the family you have now, and the family from past generations. It seeks to identify where aspects of your shadow have been created, and some find it a beneficial way to work through shadow work. Choose a practitioner who has experience in this field.

## Mandalas and Symbols

Mandalas and symbols can be found in all cultures, religions, and timelines across the world and have significance in healing and ritual practices. The practice of working with a mandala or drawing a geometric symbol helps to harmonize all aspects of the psyche—and that includes your shadow.

## Integrating the Shadow Into Your Conscious Self

All of the shadow work practices we've explored inside this book will begin the journey to integrating your shadow self. Many of these practices will help you integrate your shadow fully, especially if you keep up a continued practice of reflective journaling and mindfulness. Working through thoughts and feelings will keep you in the present moment and increase your self-awareness, preventing the shadow from growing or responding.

However, an interesting shadow technique from philosopher Ken Wilber is the 3-2-1 method (Hussain, 2020). It focuses on looking at yourself in three ways and how you fit into the world.

- In the third person, we: What do you make of the world? What's happening out there, with your friends, your wider community, and the world as a whole? What's your perception of life in general?
- In the second person, you: Consider how you interact with other people. How do friends and family see you? What would they say about you?
- In the first person, I: How do you see yourself? What do you notice about yourself? Jot down all the things about yourself that are significant.

The simplest way to imagine this process is to think of it as a puzzle, with you playing the roles of I, me, and we, just like you do in real life.

Alternatively, the Bhavana Learning Group has a very interesting way of interpreting this directly for shadow integration. Let's take a look at confronting your shadow:

1. Face them. Imagine a situation when someone was emotionally charged—this can be a positive or negative emotion.

2. Talk to them. Face this person and fix them in your mind; speak to them and connect with them and ask them how they're feeling during this emotional charge.
3. Be them. Be this person and talk about what you're going through using "I."

This can be a fun and empathetic way to reduce your shadow, and this process will help you stay calm and objective when you face challenges.

## Personal Story of Transformation

This is the story of Sadie. Sadie was abandoned by her mother at the age of five. Sadie learned quickly that she wasn't allowed to cry, as this upset her father even more. He was already devasted, and Sadie did not want to make it worse. She closed down her sadness, which also shut down part of her voice.

As a child, she became afraid to speak up. She dreaded being asked a question in school or having to talk in front of other people. She would even skip school to avoid this.

And she continued to skip many things right into adulthood.

This impacted Sadie in several different ways. She began substance abuse at the age of 14; she became an addict for 11 years. Twice during this period, she tried to take her own life, and eventually, she asked her doctor for help, and he suggested psychiatry for her.

Sadie took the clinical help and got better. But she was still afraid to be sad in front of her dad, and this created a false relationship between them. Sadie also found it difficult to speak up, even to the extent of not being able to ask for help in a local store when shopping.

Forty-three years after her mom left, Sadie finally started to do shadow work. She experienced extreme anger and rage throughout her life; in her younger years, she would get into physical altercations and argue with everyone.

She also found it difficult to sustain friendships; she felt she always said the wrong thing and had no confidence in her voice.

Sadie tried many different types of shadow work. Journaling was particularly helpful, especially when she reflected on how far she'd come.

Body scans were also her favorite for opening her heart and creating more light and power in herself, and they also made her feel relaxed after doing the deep work.

But there were aspects of herself that Saide couldn't access. After 12 months of shadow work and not being able to access her inner child, Sadie sought the help of a shadow work coach and tried several different practices to integrate her shadow. It was only after telling the story of her upbringing to her mentor that Sadie made some realizations. It was the first time that she had ever named the feeling she was experiencing and she named it "not important." As soon as she did that, they went on a guided meditation to meet her inner child, and she appeared for the first time.

Sadie was able to commute with her younger self and tell her that she was important. For weeks after this experience, Sadie saw her inner child in a few visions and dreams, and finally, her connection to this abandoned aspect of herself was being integrated. She slowly lost her sadness and rage and forgave her mom.

Out of all the practices that Sadie tried, naming her emotions was a turning point for her.

## Heartfelt Checkpoint 7

In this checkpoint, you will see another step toward emotional mastery and self-discovery. Very often when people ask you "What do you like to do for fun?" you have no idea and have to think hard about it. The next two exercises are going to work on your shadow and at the same time, identify how you can increase joy, fun, and good energy in your daily life.

## *Claim Your Emotions*

Emotional processing is something that we perhaps think about but never physically do. And naming your emotions is like calling them out. This incredible power of knowing how you feel and being able to describe it removes the personal connection to the emotion and allows you to see it as something exterior; not just a feeling you're experiencing and internalizing.

In this next interactive task, we're going to work through a range of emotions. I want you to journal which of these emotions you are feeling frequently that show up in patterns of behavior.

I want you to also journal which emotions you are fearful of feeling. We can learn so much about how we operate on a day-to-day basis when we can name the emotions that we are avoiding.

Eventually, you'll get to a point where you feel the emotion and name it, and recognizing it reduces in size and impact. This level of emotional processing expedites your journey to healing and emotional intelligence. It's something very simple but very, very effective. So, let's get started.

When looking at the emotions, see if there's one that isn't on the list and add it to your journal. Let's begin by identifying categories of emotions.

### Sad

- guilty
- ashamed
- depressed
- lonely
- bored
- tired
- remorseful
- stupid
- Inferior

- isolated
- apathetic
- sleepy

## Mad

- hurt
- hostile
- angry
- selfish
- hateful
- critical
- distant
- sarcastic
- frustrated
- jealous
- irritated
- skeptical

## Scared

- confused
- rejected
- helpless
- submissive
- insecure
- anxious
- bewildered
- discouraged
- insignificant
- inadequate
- embarrassed
- overwhelmed

## Peaceful

- content

- thoughtful
- intimate
- loving
- trusting
- nurturing
- relaxed
- pensive
- responsive
- serene
- secure
- thankful

## Powerful

- aware
- proud
- respected
- appreciated
- important
- faithful
- surprised
- successful
- worthwhile
- valuable
- discerning
- confident

## Joyful

- excited
- senseless
- energetic
- cheerful
- creative
- hopeful
- daring

- fascinating
- stimulating
- amused
- playful
- optimistic

## Step 1

First, I want you to begin with the negative emotions. List all that have been coming up for you. Some will resonate with you immediately, and you'll find yourself thinking, I feel that one; I feel that regularly! Some may be more challenging and harder to accept, and that's okay. Treat yourself with compassion as you work through this process.

## Step 2

Then, I want you to work through all the positive emotions. This is going to be a very positive process that will make you feel amazing and empowered. It will also help you identify which emotions you enjoy!

## Step 3

The next part of the task is to work through naming your emotions again, working on the negative ones first. Think back to a time or a situation where this emotion came about. Why did it arise? What triggered that feeling? Be specific.

When you finish that task, I want you to do the same with positive emotions. Look at each emotion independently and relate it to a person, task, or situation where you felt the sensation of this emotion.

The purpose of this task is important. When you can identify where you feel good emotions, you can practice more of that in your daily routine, even when you're working on your shadow. In this way, you'll be bringing light into the shadow. So, while we're accepting negative emotions, we're owning them; and by working on the positive emotions and doing more of the things you love, you're bringing so much more light into the shadow, decreasing its size and helping it dissipate.

When you can work inadvertently on your shadow by simply operating from the heart space in the things you love to do, there is no hardship, dreading, or tough days. This is another of your ultimate goals.

I'm so proud of you for undertaking this task. It's never easy looking at yourself. It's one of the hardest things that you'll ever do. But the work that you're continuing to undertake is commendable. And the things that you'll be able to achieve right now may seem unbelievable. But just watch as with each step of this workbook, you transform yourself a little bit more each time.

## *Claim Your Emotions Journaling*

As part of your ongoing self-discovery in shadow work, I want you to journal on your emotions for the next seven days.

Before going to bed each day, write down what emotions you experienced. Ask yourself how they made you feel and identify what brought about the emotion.

This is also an excellent place to note if you are not feeling any emotion. Ask yourself why you feel the absence of emotion and record your daily activities to see if there's something that you can change or do to either increase or decrease a certain emotion.

This is a seven-day task. On the seventh day, use this day for reflection and answer the following questions:

1. What patterns of emotions can I see regularly occurring within me?
2. What can I do more to increase positive feelings within myself?
3. What can I do less to decrease negative feelings in myself?
4. What is one activity that I can add to my weekly schedule that improves my joy?

## Celebration 7

Today, I want you to try something you've been longing to do but have been putting off. If it requires planning, you must agree to do it within the next seven days. Enjoy!

# CHAPTER 7

# MAINTAINING YOUR SHADOW WORK PRACTICE

When we think about positive thinking and mindfulness, we often reject the thought of diving into the dark stuff that drove us toward the need for change.

We dip in; we dip out.

And we still find that we're not quite where we want to be. We join programs, take coaching, and find healers and healing therapies.

But we regress.

We see glimpses of our shadow creeping in: An overheated argument or a jealous moment with a partner. We ghost someone on social media or run a few fake posts about ourselves. We start a new coaching program and never finish it. The list goes on. Maintenance and discipline is the key to success, and that includes shadow work.

## Creating a Long-Term Shadow Work Routine

Shadow work isn't something you can pick up and put down. It's a lifelong journey of repairing and moving forward. People, relationships, and circumstances will bring challenges to your life—that is the very essence of life. At this moment, there will be opportunities for your shadow to surface, and keeping your shadow in check will be your priority. If you don't, you will inadvertently grow your shadow—making it bigger—and all the hard work you've done will need to be unpicked again.

The tough truth is that your shadow has probably been with you for a long time. And like most people, you've also put off working on it for a long time. Or you may have started and just given up. Without the right support, shadow work can feel impossible, especially if negative thoughts and feelings surface and you start dreaming about them or feeling low. There has to be a way to pull you out of getting stuck or a pick-me-up when you begin to feel like you're falling.

## Recognizing Ongoing Shadow Issues

There are several ways to recognize if you still have your shadow showing up and preventing you from becoming the best version of yourself and succeeding in your goals.

Here are some things to look out for:

- You exhibit reactive behavior, such as jealousy or anger.
- You have impulsive behavior, such as blowing all your money and making hasty decisions without giving yourself time to think about them.
- Indecision. You're unable to make any decisions and play the waiting game.
- You have emotional outbursts or cry at the drop of a hat.
- Relationship difficulties. You choose the same partner over and over again or fall into recurring patterns of behavior in you or your love match.
- You play the victim. Are you now showing up as the victim in situations and feeling hard done by?

- Insecurities. What are you still insecure about?

- You dwell on the past. Are you spending hours lost in past experiences and thinking, What if?

- Are any big emotions surfacing regularly? What are they and how do they play a part in daily life?

- You're blocking your shadow and convincing yourself you don't have one. Everyone has one; what matters is the size of it.

- You have recurring or disturbing dreams. What's happening in your dreams?

- Your inner dialogue is negative. Are you continuing to talk yourself down and run a negative script in your head?

- Self-sabotage. Do you find yourself going so far with a person or project and then destroying your progress?

- You're labeling yourself and using labels to create your identity to avoid owning parts of yourself that need work. For example, saying you have adult ADHD or bipolar disorder when you haven't been diagnosed.

- Projecting. Are you projecting your issues by pointing out someone else's?

- Do you find yourself being defensive about your actions? Or denying that you have certain destructive behaviors?

- Are you a fake person? Are you showing up as inauthentic on social media and posting fake aspects of your life? An example of this in your character would be continuing to make the wrong connections with the wrong people.

- Are you still a perfectionist? Maybe you never finish projects or tasks because you have to get them better and better and they never see completion.

- What about addiction? Overeating, alcohol, or substance abuse. Porn addiction or gambling? Obsessively working out or going to the gym? What addiction can you pinpoint in your life?

- Time deficient. Are you telling yourself you are too busy and have no time; unable to make time for short spurts of regular self-care work?

If any one of the points struck a chord with you or you could immediately say, "Yes! I still do that," then it's likely that shadow work needs to be regularly continued.

And don't worry, you are not the only one.

Spend a few moments now thinking of the close people in your life. What can you identify about their personalities that show you they have shadow work to do, too? This will help you feel less isolated and alone. After all, everyone has a shadow, but only some take the responsibility and courage to change it.

## Balancing Shadow Work With Self-Care

If you think about bad things all the time, you're going to feel bad.

And that goes for shadow work too. You can't think about the things you want to change about yourself without bolstering yourself with powerful, empowering work, too.

If you don't, you'll stop doing the work and just feel bad.

Period.

So, instead of teaching a balanced shadow work self-care approach, let's build one together.

Start here by choosing one of the shadow work practices and then coupling it with a self-care practice:

1. Journal about five negative beliefs, then write five positive affirmations about yourself.
2. Explore past trauma, then create five gratitude statements.
3. Call out your triggers, then sink into a mindfulness guided meditation.
4. Find repressed emotions and journal on them, then choose one

form of creative expression and go do it.

5. Identify recurring patterns in relationships, then call a friend and go for an empathy walk.

6. Observe negative inner dialogue, write it down, and then reframe each negative sentence positively.

7. Work with your inner child. Write a letter to them to tell them what you love and have learned about yourself.

8. Work through limiting beliefs, then set three goals to achieve within three months.

9. Identify unconscious bias by learning something new about another culture or volunteering.

10. Face your fears through self-reflection journaling to celebrate your bravery and acknowledge your accomplishments.

Balance is the key to success in anything in life, and you'll see that the more you nurture yourself with an exercise that promotes self-love and increased self-awareness, the easier it will be to stay on track with your shadow work.

# Heartfelt Checkpoint 8
## *Self-Date*

The second part of our heartfelt checkpoint is to take yourself on a self-date.

This entails taking a shower, putting on your nicest outfit, and taking yourself, alone, for a coffee or a slice of cake or somewhere where you can spend some time to appreciate and celebrate yourself.

It doesn't matter where you go, but you should take the time to get yourself ready. Pamper yourself and then go and celebrate yourself.

This exercise is a deeply empowering exercise that also increases confidence.

Remember to journal about how you felt before your date and how you felt after it, too.

Not only will you have a great time, but you will increase your self-worth and emotional intelligence.

## Celebration 8

Today, you have already celebrated yourself, so now I want you to plan a big celebration for the completion of this workbook. Go big! Invite friends and family and share your experience.

# CHAPTER 8
# RELATIONSHIPS AND SHADOW WORK

Relationships and shadow work are boldly intertwined.

They are often the very thing that brings the shadow out into the open; and anything that brings forth the shadow can end up in overreaction, impulsivity, emotional outbursts, and projecting when faced with a challenging person or situation.

The biggest relationship that the shadow will overtake is the one you have with yourself. And like Dr. Jekyll and Mr. Hyde, the shadow can overtake you if you're not careful. The shadow is easy to identify in relationships because it usually brings up negative or toxic behaviors. These can be such things as jealousy, rage, love-bombing, indecision, and many more character facets that can be noticeably regarded as out-of-control or intense emotions. They can be classed as out of the ordinary, over the top, obsessive, impulsive, or reactive.

The shadow can also bring about the victim. You may hear victim phrases like "Why are you always doing this to me?" "Why don't they love me?" "Why do bad things always happen to me?" and many more. The shadow isn't just the pieces of negative emotions— negative emotions also have positive aspects. The shadow is pieces of you that can arise in every situation and every relationship. Be it love, work, children, family, your relationship with food, alcohol, TV, and social media. Your shadow shows up in every single part of your life. There is no place for you to hide.

There is only one solution, and that is to work on reducing your shadow. So, let's dive deep into shadow work and relationships to see if we can navigate a way to allow the best version of yourself to come forward at all times. If we accept the shadow is always there, it prevents us from being naive and blocking more behaviors. You are going to love and embrace your shadow, that's the simplest way to reduce it. And when it does show up, you're going to deal with it calmly and mindfully because you know what the shadow is going to do next. Nobody knows your shadow better than you, and that's your weapon in taming it!

## How the Shadow Effects Relationships

So, before we look at how the shadow affects relationships, let's first look at how the shadow shows up in relationships. See if you can identify one or a few of these ways of the shadow. Has your shadow popped up and attracted a certain type of partner? Think back to previous partners you've had. What exactly have you been attracted to?

- Have you been attracted to their childhood trauma? Was it similar to yours?

- Have you been attracted to a piece of their personality that you don't have like, for example, assertiveness? Maybe you want to see this in yourself and don't, but this quality mostly ends up becoming a trigger.

- Have you been attracted to anger and aggression? Because you want to release that anger and aggression to deal with the terrible trauma you've been through and you don't know how to deal with it.

These are all aspects of your shadow attracting their shadow. This is dangerously deceptive because when your shadow is attracted to another, it's wrapped up in a lot of negativity, conflict, and pain. Very often, those are the only things you're going to feel in that relationship, which leads straight to disaster.

## Projection

Your shadow can also affect relationships through projection. When we have feelings of repressed anger deep down inside of us, we make the smallest disagreements everybody else's fault. And usually, that hits the closest person to us. We can destroy relationships through constant arguing, bickering, and conflict. And that's the shadow inside of us doing it. It's not us. It's the things from the past that you're still bringing forward into the present. This past experience means nothing in your present life, but every time we are triggered by it, we bring that shadow forward and increase its size.

## Childhood Style

A popular belief held by some is that love relationships will always seek to mirror your childhood. For example, if you're always searching for the childhood you didn't have, you'll be unconsciously looking for it in your relationships. If you had areas of conflict growing up, then it's likely that you will bring those forward into your current relationships, even friendships, work relationships, and most definitely love relationships.

## Self-Sabotage

Another way that the shadow shows up in relationships is self-sabotage. You may have been chasing the partner of your dreams. You may have won over that partner, and you may be in a loving relationship. But deep down, if you don't feel that you deserve the relationship and the love that goes with it, your shadow will seek to destroy it at every opportunity. This is typical of the shadow when there are feelings of low self-esteem and low self-worth. Your shadow will act out ways to destroy your relationship, create conflict, and bring you back to your most comfortable emotional state of low self-esteem and rejection.

## *Inauthentic Relationships*

Fake relationships are a big thing. When the shadow is showing up in your daily life, you may think you're presenting the authentic version of yourself. But when the shadow is in control, you are presenting somebody who's inauthentic. Fake relationships can happen in love, work, and friendships. And what happens to relationships based on inauthenticity is that they fall apart quickly. The cracks begin to show, and when you spend more time with others, they start to realize that you are not who you appear to be.

These can be attributed to the shadow, and because you never seem to be able to maintain friendships, you can slip into the belief you can't make friends. This isn't true. But the missing pieces of your character need to be integrated for you to have genuine, authentic relationships with genuine, whole people.

## *Communication Difficulty*

The shadow also shows up if you have difficulty communicating when you can't express yourself to your partner, your children, or your loved ones. Doubt becomes an area of strain within a relationship when things go unsaid. It can create resentment, disappointment, and a lack of connection, and all of those things lead to the breakdown of the relationship. This is primarily caused by the shadow, and the longer the problem exists, the greater the shadow grows.

## Navigating Conflicts and Improving Communication

Undertaking shadow work can give you huge benefits in managing disagreements and enhancing dialogue. Work through the ways below; and in your journal, write down which ones you would find the easiest to work with to make a conscious decision in approaching conflict differently next time:

## *Switch "You" to "I"*

When the shadow has been at work, causing mischief, conflict, and creating distance between two people, it's sometimes hard to find a resolution with words. However, one of the key ways to talk to somebody after you've argued is to change the way you frame your sentences. For example, instead of saying "you," change that to "I." In this way, you put yourself at the center of the conversation, instead of making the other person feel like the target and as though they are being attacked. This also helps you to avoid projection, too.

## *Journaling*

Another important way to get to the bottom of why you have conflict in a relationship is to start journaling on the problems that keep surfacing. Very often, we think that when there is a problem between two people, it's the other person's fault. Journaling is the best way to look at yourself deeply; it's a private space for you to reflect and grow. You can ask yourself any questions and be honest about how you feel inside. It remains an underrated practice with huge benefits.

## *Mirrored Traits*

When the shadow is at work, we are very often mirroring a character trait that shows up in somebody else. And that's exacerbated by the denial of that character trait within ourselves. So, we get angrier and angrier when we see this personality flaw represented in another human being because we dislike it so much in ourselves. This is evident in relationships with children. When we have a child who exposes key personality characteristics we hold and we've tried to either eradicate or disown them, this can send us into a mind-blowing rage within ourselves. We love our children so much that we don't want to see this negative part of their personality in them, especially because we passed it down, and now we feel responsible for it!

So, this is where a lot of conflict can arise in families. A really good way to combat this is through talking and verbalization. Talking through problems, sharing, and trying to find a resolution is the number one way to deal with any problem, trauma, or issue that causes distress.

## Conflict Resolution

However, I appreciate that that's hard to do sometimes and even harder with the closest people to you. Especially when you see each other day in and day out. If it's impossible to find a resolution and get to that sweet spot that makes your family and loved ones tick, then try conflict resolution with a therapist or a mediator. What this does is help you create the space to listen to one another without making yourself the center of the issue.

For example, if you can listen to a problem from someone else's perspective, this induces empathy. Understanding how they feel and how the situation affects them increases your self-awareness and helps you to understand a wider view of the problem. If you can acknowledge somebody else's criticism without reacting or slipping into impulsive, explosive behavior, this helps you get to the bottom of the issue faster. It also helps you to deal with problems similar to this in the future. There are problems in every family structure, relationship, and situation, but it's how you deal with them that matters. Calmly talking things through without apportioning blame is the best way to try and find a resolution without increasing your shadow.

## Increase Your Vulnerability

One of the hardest things to do in times of conflict is to be vulnerable in front of someone else. However, opening your heart in front of a loved one is something you should practice. Vulnerability helps to foster a connection between two people and breaks down barriers when anger, resentment, or fear stand in the way of good communication. Being vulnerable takes time, and the best way to increase this quality within yourself is to practice in small baby steps. In this way, you get to open your heart more, bit by bit, and let people into your heart space. You will find that in return, people will be vulnerable with you. Conflict and disagreements will be much easier to resolve. They won't get to the stage where emotional blowouts happen.

## Setting Boundaries

Setting boundaries is also another important way to resolve conflicts and improve communication. Make sure that you have your standards in check. Having standards about the way you want to be treated reflects your self-worth and increases your self-esteem. Be mindful not to make boundaries that are so firm that you cut people off. This also increases the shadow because it's blocking and not dealing with the problem. Another way to look at it is that everybody deserves a chance and everybody makes mistakes. We are all human. But it's good to understand when you've reached your limit with another person and when it's time to say no and move on.

## Practice Forgiveness

Practicing forgiveness is perhaps the number one way to improve communication. When the shadow has been at work, forgiveness seeks to release you from the burden of the problem. Never think that because you forgive another, the other person gets let off the hook or doesn't face consequences. Forgiveness is a gift you give yourself. Otherwise, you hold the anger, disappointment, jealousy, or resentment inside of you. This makes the shadow bigger and bigger and increases the space between you and improved emotional intelligence.

Forgiving yourself is always the first place to start when you practice forgiveness. Then, you can move on to forgiving others within your life. Remember that people make mistakes when they don't know any better at the time. You will have done this too; we all do. Accepting this stops you from holding the weight of others' actions, and acceptance permits you to release yourself from any bad feelings.

## Practicing Patience

Have you ever wondered how some people are patient while others aren't? Patience is a skill that needs to be practiced. You will often see that mothers have an abundance of patience because they have practiced it over and over again with small children. When we have behaved badly, we long for patience and acceptance from another person, so why are we so bad at giving it ourselves? Being patient is not something that will happen overnight; but if you commit to the practice, you will be proud of yourself, and you'll find that others admire this quality in you, too.

Practicing patience is the gift you give yourself that increases your emotional intelligence. Your shadow self will always want you to react, explode, and be impulsive and not think about the consequences. And there will be an internal struggle when you begin to practice it.

Practicing patience takes time. But when you start being patient with others, you'll find you have that returned to you, as the energy you emit will attract the same energy back. It's a great weapon to have in your arsenal against your shadow, as the work you do on yourself will be the greatest key to unlocking and improving communication methods.

If you continue to practice self-awareness by journaling and mindfulness activities, you will see that you will naturally become a better communicator. You will be calmer, and you will think instead of emotionally reacting when you want to discuss a problem. Self-awareness is your greatest asset. It's also one of the shadow's biggest fears, so the more you improve this quality within yourself, the greater your ability to fight anything in life and gain more confidence in the process.

## Healing Relationships Through Shadow Work

The amazing thing about shadow work is that it increases compassion. Your expansion in compassion will, in turn, help you to see things from your partner's point of view. This is important in healing relationships. Oftentimes, you'll find that when conflict is in a relationship, distance increases between two people. And working through your shadow work will help you to decrease that distance. It will bring you closer together. As a by-product of all the work you do in your shadow, your personal growth will expand and bring a positive impact to all relationships. If you remember, relationships are based on everything in life: work, money, food, health, community, and personal life. Your energy is your greatest asset, but it can be your worst enemy. Remember to nurture it.

It's also worth noting that while nobody wants to be called out and have their shadow work identified, it does give you the compassion to see when others haven't worked on theirs. This also gives you the ability to help them when they're going through a dark time and perhaps redirect them to something that will help them manage their emotions better.

But perhaps the most important thing to note is healing the relationship within yourself. You'll find that once you're on the right track with your shadow work, everything in your life will become a lot easier. There will be more ease in your work, home life, and your family and the day-to-day will become a lot more enjoyable.

## Heartfelt Checkpoint 9

In this heartfelt checkpoint, I want you to write a letter of forgiveness to yourself.

First, we will go through some examples of things you could forgive yourself for.

Then, we will create seven statements of forgiveness as examples. After that, I want you to go on to create your own statements that are personal to you.

Remember that these will change over time. Maybe once a month, you can look at refreshing the seven areas you want to forgive yourself for. This will keep you constantly evolving and decreasing your shadow. Let's begin.

1. **Forgive yourself for poor decisions.** Think back to when you made a bad decision. What was happening in your life at the time? Were you trying to please somebody else? Were you

trying to keep the peace or was it just a simple error of judgement? Everybody makes mistakes. Looking at those mistakes, owning them, and seeing how you could have made a better judgment will help you move forward. It also really pushes your personal growth in the right direction.

2. **Forgive yourself for being your own worst critic.** No one will give you a hard time like you will. Forgiveness work provides major transformation and a turning point in your shadow work journey. By forgiving yourself, you will reframe statements or the negative dialogue that comes up when you start giving yourself a hard time.

3. **Forgive yourself for feeling regret.** Regret is a feeling that does not serve us in any way, and missed opportunities are just part of life. Fear often plays a part in us not seizing the day, and maybe this opportunity wasn't right for you at the time. Opportunity is always evolving throughout your life. Just because you missed one opportunity doesn't mean that you'll miss another. Forgive yourself for feeling regret and stay in the present moment.

4. **Forgive yourself for the time when you didn't know better.** This usually comes up in abusive and toxic relationships. Show forgiveness for not having stronger self-worth, knowing that you are worth more than being treated like a doormat or a punching bag. Forgive yourself for not feeling important and showing yourself the love that you deserve. Acknowledge that you did your best at that time.

5. **Use forgiveness to be compassionate about unrealistic expectations you've set for yourself.** We all expected to be further on than we are now. Forgive yourself for feeling that way. And know that just by doing these exercises, you are moving in the right direction now.

6. **Forgive yourself for negative inner dialogue and negative beliefs.** Forgive yourself for not attracting positive beliefs and positive things in your life. Forgive yourself for hindering your

progress. Know that you won't do that again.

7. **Forgive yourself for not loving yourself enough and neglecting yourself.** You are the most important person to you, and no one loves you more than you will love yourself. Forgive yourself for not putting the correct food in your body, for not working your muscles correctly, for not connecting with nature. Forgive yourself and make sure that you are mindful of all those things in the present moment.

Next, look at the seven statement examples created below and say these before your affirmations each day.

### *My Forgiveness Letter—Example*

1. I forgive myself for my bad decisions when I did not know any better.
2. I forgive myself for verbally beating myself up.
3. I forgive myself for feeling the regret of missed opportunities.
4. I forgive myself for lowering my standards in toxic relationships.
5. I forgive myself for putting expectations on myself.
6. I forgive myself for my negative thoughts and beliefs.
7. I forgive myself for neglecting myself.

Now, it's your time to create your own and say these before your affirmations each day.

## Celebration 9

Forgiveness work is tough. Today, I want self-care to be optimized. Run a big bubble bath and soak, listening to your favorite soothing music.

# CHAPTER 9
# ADVANCED SHADOW WORK TECHNIQUES

There is no one way to use shadow work to help you retrieve those lost pieces of yourself. We all veer toward different practices and rituals. The most important thing for you is to find one that you enjoy—that way you'll feel positive and excited about doing the work, which will keep you consistent and accountable. If you find a practice that you really don't enjoy, move on and explore another. And if you want to go even deeper, keep on listening.

## Exploring Deeper Layers of the Shadow

During our time working through this workbook, we haven't considered how our shadow affects society at large. We've looked deeply at the layer of the shadow that affects us the most. We've looked at where it comes in to disturb our relationships with every part of our life, including health, wealth, and love. What we haven't explored yet is the deeper layer of the shadow that forms part of the collective shadow.

We enter this world with unconscious bias, which begins forming in our childhood with the effects coming from the society we live in. This means that we may not be consciously aware of our bias toward certain things. The culture we've grown up in gets instilled inside of us from an early age. For example, we may believe that people from developed countries are somewhat more civilized than those from developing countries. This happens in areas of race, religion, and many other areas of life. This isn't something that you can control. But being aware of it can help you reduce your reaction toward other races, cultures, religions, and other people in society at large.

When you feel an aversion to something, this is your shadow at work. And in this age of information, we are often given a lot of incorrect facts and media-biased opinions. It's important to be mindful of what we allow into our intellect, as biased opinion is set to unbalance us.

But there are always great ways to tackle this and educate yourself. You can travel to places you usually wouldn't or immerse yourself in volunteering or in simply learning about other countries, cultures, religions, and traditions. So, when you experience anything different from what you know and are comfortable with, you react in a very balanced manner with a much broader view of the world. This helps to reduce the collective shadow. While the collective shadow may seem enormous, if everybody can do their piece of work to reduce it, then we will all have a better world to live in.

Addressing unconscious bias will help you unlock stereotypes, diversity, inclusion, and equality; don't undervalue its effects on yourself or your community.

## Working With Dreams and Symbols

Working with dreams and symbols to work through your shadow requires a very open mind.

Sometimes, it takes you to a different level within yourself. It can connect with your spiritual core and help to express pieces of your higher self and different levels of creativity. It can also be confusing and disturbing if not done in the right way. So, it's important to counterbalance working with dreams and symbols together with self-care practices.

You could begin by starting a dream journal, paying attention only to the emotions in your dreams. Write your dreams down regularly and see if you can find a pattern or reoccurring emotions that come up for you. Interpretation of these emotions is going to be subjective, and I recommend that you have a very balanced approach to interpreting what they may mean and get the help of a specialist if you need it—especially if you encounter areas that are worrying or make you feel uncomfortable.

Inside your dreams, you're often going to come across different animals, places, and people. And these can be viewed as symbolic depending on the culture and tradition you value. Symbols mean different things in different cultures and traditions, and perhaps here it's important to take a holistic view of what these symbols mean to you.

Never become obsessed or dwell on the negative aspects of these symbols; symbolism will give you both positive and negative viewpoints. If you inadvertently dwell on negative parts of symbolism, this is going to increase your shadow, and it's not going to help you. However, if you always look at symbols as something like a guideline or an indication of something positive, then that's a very healthy approach.

Remember, you will always find what you're looking for. If you're looking for deeper significance in something, you will always find it. We are attracted to what we think about, and this works in both positive and negative ways.

If you enjoy exploring your dreams, then it's quite easy to do. Sink into a meditative state by closing your eyes and going on an active journey back inside your dream to see what you can find, what resonates with you, and what helps you reach the resolution you are looking for.

I would stress that it is important to stay on top of positive significance and symbolism. If your shadow shows up in your dream as an aggressive person, a bad situation, or trauma, take a deep breath and try to engage with this person or this situation and ask it questions. Ask what it is trying to tell you to see if you can unpick the process in your mind. Your mind is taking you on this journey for a reason. What is it trying to say?

During your dream visitation, if you find aspects of yourself that you believe need to be integrated, go ahead and do so. Embrace these pieces of yourself with compassion and love. See if this is another doorway to working through your shadow work in a very positive manner.

Many therapists and alternative practitioners work with dream therapies. If you need help in this area or you want to go deeper, it's a great idea to get professional help and never be afraid to ask.

# Shamanic and Therapeutic Approaches

Shamanic approaches steer you more toward the spiritualist side of shadow work. It's up to you to decide if this is something you want to explore and find a connection with. Let's go a little deeper:

## *Shamanic Approaches*

Shamanic approaches to shadow work provide a different level of exploring your shadow. Many of these practices involve meditation. If you take shamanic journeying, for example, this is where you use music, or repeated rhythms like the beat of a drum, to go back on a journey to find aspects of your shadow. This takes you deep into your unconscious and helps you retrieve pieces of yourself that you have once denied or been ashamed of. Some call it soul retrieval.

This can be a deeply healing way to retrieve parts of your psyche, and it requires quite a lot of energy to partake in these rituals. Before you go headfirst into shamanic journeying, make sure that you are feeling well and that your energy level is high. You may feel a little depleted after doing this work. It's also worth bearing in mind that when you do any deep energy work, it can take a day or even a week to recover.

As part of shamanic approaches, you can also delve into the practice of animal work. This work is usually called animal guides. Animals represent a deep connection to the natural world, the original world where you began. Animals here are used in many different ways as symbols or as presentation of certain personality traits. Other animals are viewed as protectors or totems. You may even find yourself with an animal guide who will steer you and your shadow into the light.

Again, most of these practices will be through guided meditation or ritual, and you must balance this kind of work with lots of self-care. While exploration can provide deep insights into your psyche, and your shadow, it can also be uncomfortable and unsettling at times. You may feel slightly imbalanced when you finish doing this work. If you explore this journey, you must do it with a lot of time and compassion for recovery. Not everyone reacts in the same way to shamanic work and a deeply meditative state, so you must make sure you can feel and see a physical tether to the present world in the present moment. If you don't come out of deep mind exploration experiences properly, you can feel disconnected and foggy.

## *Therapeutic Approaches*

Alternative therapies can be very simple approaches to healing the shadow. Let's explore some of those here, and while you thinking about them, see how they feel in your body as we go through each one:

## *Psychotherapy*

Several therapeutic approaches are very interesting. One of them is psychotherapy. In this practice, you can go back in time and act out certain parts of your childhood to see what comes up and what emotions you felt as a child. Your relationship with time was very different from the relationship you have with time now. For example, one week may have felt like 12 months as a child, so unwrapping and unpicking things that happened in your childhood in a safe space can help you get a lot of clarity and shift some limiting beliefs that have helped to create your shadow.

## Talking Therapy

Simple talking therapy is another way for you to express withheld or repressed emotions. By spending time with another person talking over your fears, emotional outbursts, and feelings, you can get to the heart of many problems and trace their roots, making them easier to dissipate. In the society that we live in now, we do very little "real talk" about the things that cause us a problem and affect the way that we live. With the constantly increasing use of social media, we have turned into a very inauthentic society that, on a collective level, has increased the collective shadow. That rebounds on us and increases our shadow. So, while talking therapy may seem like a very simple option, it's very, very therapeutic.

## Art Therapy

Art therapy is a very popular way of expressing yourself in a nonverbal sense. Over the years, this therapy has become very popular because it provides release in artistic expression. This means that you can paint or draw anything you want to, as it's an expression of art, and free yourself of the dark side of your shadow in a beautiful context. This is often met with less judgment than if you were talking about the same emotional experience. Immersing yourself in therapy also gives you the time to disconnect from your thoughts. And if it's something you love, it's a beautiful act of self-care at the same time.

## Gestalt Therapy

Gestalt therapy is also a therapeutic approach where you avoid going into past experiences and stay in the present. You may be worried or nervous about an upcoming task or event, and this may bring some feelings to you that you need to explore. A trained therapist will help you do that by staying in the present moment and talking about your feelings surrounding your worry. Bringing these out into the open helps you get more clarity on what's happening to you and why it's happening, and it helps you to neutralize and manage your feelings in a better way.

# Heartfelt Checkpoint 10

In the last section of this book, we've been looking at alternative ways of exploring shadow work. One of these ways can be with artistic expression. In this final checkpoint, we're going to make the aspects of your shadow into characters.

## *Creative Shadow Characters*

One of the most fun ways of doing shadow work is by making your shadow aspects into real characters. And you are going to give all the characters in your shadow a voice!

You will create characters for each one of your shadow elements and turn them into real people. This is a fun way to visualize the aspects of your shadow. You can even give them names and call them out when you feel that they're starting to rise within you.

Adding humor to painful aspects of life is a great way of dealing with challenging aspects of yourself. When you're lighthearted about facets of your character, you're eager to change, and it makes the process a lot sweeter. Step by step, we're going to dive into character exploration, and this helps you to externalize your shadow rather than internalize its negativity.

### Step 1

Identify the pieces of your shadow. These can be anything from repressed emotions, fears, desires, inabilities, silence, or any aspects of your shadow that have been showing up for you. Write them down now.

### Step 2

It's time to give your shadow aspects a name. Think about how they look. What physical features do they have? What other personality traits? Once you've identified these create a background story for each one. If you need to meditate on this that can be a fun way to do it. What's the backstory of this character? Who are they? What kind of life do they live? What kind of hopes and dreams does this character have?

## Step 3

Create a short story. Once you have identified your characters and named them and you can see a picture of them in your head, it's time to create either a monologue or a short story about them. A monologue, for example, would be something typical that your shadow aspect would say. What kinds of words and phrases do they use? How do they express themselves? What are they thinking about? What do they fear? What do they desire? What are their dreams and goals?

You can also write a short story about them. What happened to this character? Where have they been? What have they suffered? What have they done to other people? Go through all their experiences, and keep it as amusing as possible.

## Step 4

If you are creative, then paint a picture of your character. Draw them, paint them, or make a clay model of them. By doing this, it's again externalizing your shadow aspects and bringing beauty and light into them.

## Step 5

What does your character want to achieve? What are they trying to express? How are they trapped inside? What's keeping them there? What's stopping them from moving forward and into the light?

## Step 6

It's time for reflection. Now, how do these characters relate to you? Can you see a tie or a tether between you? What's your connection?

How is this character playing out in your life? What would you like to see happen to this character? Usually by thinking about your character as someone else, it's easier to see a clearer vision of how their life should be lived beautifully.

**Step 7**

Now, you need to integrate this character. You know everything about them, what they do, why they react, what they want from life, and how are they going to get there. It's time to integrate them into yourself. You can do this through simple visualization or meditation. Spend time with them in your head. Make them feel loved because, after all, you're just loving pieces of yourself.

**Step 8**

Share your character. Find a community or share with friends and family how you explored your shadow work using this creative process. It will be really fun and interesting to hear if your family, friends, or community members use this form of artistic expression. This can provide a refreshing sense of release in an area of personal growth that is undoubtedly the hardest. We know that when we bring humor and light to the darkest of times, they're much easier to deal with, and this is a perfect way to explore an alternative practice of shadow work.

## *Take the 30-Day Shadow Challenge*

Engaging in the 30-day shadow work challenge is going to make you feel motivated and inspired in an alternative way to address your biggest challenges!

### Week 1—Self-Discovery

**Day 1:** Journal on your current state of emotions and where you are in your shadow work progress.

**Day 2:** Engage in a meditation of your choice for at least 15 minutes to establish your level of self-awareness.

**Day 3:** Set an intention. Choose one shadow aspect you would like to work on over the next 30 days.

**Day 4:** Stay grounded. Take part in breathwork, yoga, or any exercise or physical activity of your choice that makes you feel good.

**Day 5:** Tell a friend about your 30-day challenge and see if you can get them to join you.

**Day 6:** Make one affirmation specifically on self-acceptance. Pin it on a wall or somewhere you can repeat it at least three times a day.

**Day 7:** Spend some time outdoors reflecting on the week and your progress so far. Try and connect with nature.

## Week 2—Connecting With Your Shadow

**Day 8:** Write a letter to yourself acknowledging the different parts of your shadow that you are currently aware of.

**Day 9:** Take a journey to meet your inner child. See how they're feeling and try and find out if they are directly connected to aspects of your shadow.

**Day 10:** Take part in the artistic expression of your shadow through writing, dancing, or music.

**Day 11:** Write a letter to someone you need to forgive. You don't need to send it, but write the letter for yourself.

**Day 12:** Learn something new about shadow work. Use the free resources on the internet or take part in a workshop where you can be active and present.

**Day 13:** Practice gratitude. Shadow work can make you feel low at times; balance that out with at least seven statements of gratitude.

**Day 14:** Look closely at your shadow aspects and see if you can identify any positives in the negative traits of your shadow.

## Week 3—Integration

**Day 15:** Try a meditation on integrating parts of your shadow. Visualize yourself welcoming in aspects of your shadow.

**Day 16:** Try to explore or at least research something new that aligns with the potential your shadow aspect could have.

**Day 17:** List all the people who trigger your shadow and start to create boundaries for them.

**Day 18:** Look into getting more support from a mentor or a guide. If you need a free resource, go to YouTube and find a personal growth specialist, shadow work healer, or psychologist with whom you vibe.

**Day 19:** Write a letter to your future self. Tell them about the person you want to be.

**Day 20:** Work out, exercise, or do something that makes your heart rate increase and disconnects your mind from your body. This will help you release any emotions you are struggling with.

**Day 21:** Practice affirmations of acceptance. Create five affirmations about accepting where you are now and loving yourself as you are today.

## Week 4—Growth

**Day 22:** Create a new vision board representing the desires of the person you want to be when your shadow work is complete and your shadow is as small as possible.

**Day 23:** Explore personal growth to greater depths. Which mentor do you resonate with? Start one of their programs and work through their books and videos.

**Day 24:** Practice random acts of kindness. Do something for someone else today. Even if you can only manage to smile or say hello to someone, engage in something for no personal gratification at all.

**Day 25:** Journal how you've come on this road and what parts of your shadow have now transformed.

**Day 26:** Share your experience online in a community or with your family or friends.

**Day 27:** What action can you take today to integrate the piece of your shadow that you are working on? Name that action.

**Day 28:** Reflect on all of your journal entries from the beginning of this challenge and celebrate yourself. Go for a coffee, go to a restaurant, go to the cinema, or book a holiday—whatever it is, celebrate yourself today!

**Day 29:** What self-care does your new version of yourself need? Make a list and practice one thing on that list.

**Day 30:** Write a letter to the person you were on day one. Thank them for taking part in this challenge. Thank them for growing and not being fearful and acknowledge their strength along this journey.

## Celebration 10

Wow! Look how far you've come! Treat yourself to a spa day in total relaxation and reward for a job well done.

# CONCLUSION

This workbook has taken you on a journey through your own shadow work. Well done for making it to the end!

I hope that during your shadow work practice, you have undertaken equal amounts of self-care to counterbalance bringing out and dissipating the dark side of yourself.

Remember that shadow work is an ongoing journey. This work is never complete. It would be wonderful to feel that there would never be another challenge or problematic person you would face for the rest of your life, but that's a dream. It is your job now to make sure that your shadow decreases and doesn't grow.

You can hide from your shadow. You can pretend it's not there. But remember those things grow your shadow. The best way forward now is to be completely responsible for keeping it as small as possible and bring in as much light into yourself to keep your shadow at bay.

From the very first chapter of this workbook, you started a process of transformation. What levels of transformation can you now see in yourself? Are you pausing to think before you speak? Are you taking a deep breath when an emotion arises? Are you an observer, watching an emotion rise, observing it, and then letting it float on by?

If so, this is a huge transformation and milestone, and I congratulate you on the personal growth that you now have achieved. This is the evolution of you; the evolution of your spirit and your soul. And as long as you keep practicing those rituals, you will keep on evolving and creating increased emotional intelligence.

When we have talked about integration, what have you managed to integrate? Have you integrated pieces of your inner child? Maybe you've managed to integrate your inner child completely. Have you integrated anger and jealousy and know that the next time that they both show up, you're not going to let them run the show? Integration is the absolute goal of shadow work. And now it's time to see what goals and dreams you can achieve in this new, whole version of yourself.

Shadow work is a lifelong exploration of the challenges of your dark side. Remember, there is nothing wrong with having a dark side. We have to have dark to have light; we have to have night to have day. But what we don't want is your shadow to ever take over the best version of yourself. We want to keep on receiving abundance. Keep on achieving goals. Keep on living life on your terms, the way we imagine it should be.

If you've reached the end and feel anything less than amazing, I would encourage you to spend more time in practices of self-love, self-esteem, self-worth, and self-care. This will increase your self-awareness, and you will create more compassion for yourself; the byproduct of this is your happiness.

Don't feel that you are alone on this journey. Everyone who undertakes shadow work does so knowing that this is the beginning of a road that never ends. You are brave, you are strong, and you can do this. Even if you have only taken one step in this direction, you have taken one more step that millions of other people haven't.

Maybe you're feeling now it's time to share your experiences or you need further support. Find a community that can hold space for you. If that's not enough, don't forget you can always seek out professional help. Combining professional help with therapies and practices we've already discussed is a great idea to move forward. Don't ever think of working on yourself as something negative. Those of us who want to move past our struggles and move forward in life with increased emotional intelligence are the ones who will succeed in health, wealth, and relationships.

So, now I'm curious to know what new goals you have. What can you achieve now that you couldn't when you started this workbook? Remember the big question: If there was no fear, what would you do with your life? How would you answer that differently now? Does that question feel exciting rather than scary? I'm excited about your future, and I hope it's one that you're excited about, too.

Before we close this chapter of your shadow work, remember to use this book whenever you want. Make it a point to journal about it in three months, six months, or even once a year to keep you on track. And don't forget to share it with your friends if you see them struggling with a shadow aspect they cannot shift.

Before we go, we're going to explore a questionnaire similar to the one that we did when you started the book. This is a perfect time for you to reflect on just how far you've come from day one. I bet it's miles further than you ever imagined!

## Self-Discovery Transformation

Take the self-discovery questionnaire to document your transformation and take you to the next level of completeness!

1. What is your perception of yourself now?
2. What have you learned about yourself on this shadow work journey?
3. How is your self-awareness now different?
4. Has your shadow been triggered since the beginning of this

book?

5. Did you find any recurring patterns of behavior in your shadow work? Are they still present in your life now?

6. Which parts of your shadow work have been the hardest?

7. What did you not enjoy delving into and how did you work through these?

8. Name three breakthroughs you had during the book. How have they impacted your life?

9. Can you identify any major changes in current relationships after working through this book? How does that make you feel?

10. What is the one technique you learned from this workbook that you are going to continue to practice?

11. What is the one technique that you did not enjoy from this workbook? And what does that tell you about yourself? Is that something that you can identify in your shadow?

12. How difficult was it to forgive yourself during the book? Does thinking about forgiving yourself still make you feel emotional?

13. What is now your favorite self-awareness practice?

14. What is now your favorite self-love practice?

15. Are your goals and dreams now clearer or different from when you began?

16. Do you have something that you want to aim for that was different from when you started the book?

17. Have you created a schedule where you have equal shadow work and self-care practices scheduled regularly?

18. Are there any new techniques you want to try but you are unsure of trying?

19. What advice would you give to someone starting their shadow work? Could you help them in any way?

20. What has been your biggest integration and is there anything left you feel you need to integrate?

## *Seven-Day Self-Care Checklist for Your Onward Journey*

You didn't think I'd leave you here without helping you maintain all the good work, did you?

Let's create your checklist to keep you going strong in the days ahead!

**Day 1:** Spend time reflecting on how far you've come in your shadow work journey. Write a letter to yourself today that celebrates your courage and determination for your personal growth. Write down another aspect of your shadow that you want to explore in the future.

**Day 2:** Make a gratitude list today, especially taking into account the positive changes that have come from your recent shadow work. Write a self-appreciation list, identifying at least seven qualities or strengths that you've discovered as a result of this shadow work.

**Day 3:** Be mindful. Engage in any mindfulness activity that makes you feel good. It can be mindful breathing, mindfulness meditation, an empathy walk, or talking with a friend. Simply mindfully explore your thoughts and feelings by observation of your inner self today. You should pamper yourself with self-love and a comforting activity that makes you feel good and gives you space to think about something else.

**Day 4:** Get involved in a community project or work that encompasses shadow work. Talk to a friend about their journey. Talk to your family and see if they need help with that.

**Day 5:** Create a ritual for yourself. releasing parts of the shadow or letting go of people in your life who trigger the shadow. Say goodbye to things from your past. Find a way of letting go. That could be exercise, writing, and burning a letter. Throwing stones in the river, anything you choose shows you that you have released and let go.

**Day 6:** This is your celebration day. Treat yourself to a meal, take yourself out for a coffee, go for a walk, or get out in nature. Think about how positive your life could be if you continue on this path of growth.

**Day 7:** Set some goals and intentions for the future that align with your future self. Spend some time in nature and reconnect with the earth. Ground yourself; anchor yourself to all that is and all that you want to be.

I leave you in love and light and peace for the future. Good luck with your onward journey to being the best version of yourself.

# REFERENCES


Aletheia. (2020, April 25). *Breathwork: 11 magical techniques for spiritual healing.* LonerWolf. https://lonerwolf.com/breathwork/#h-5-intensely-transformative-types-of-breathwork

Cherry, K. (2021, April 24). *Why self-esteem is important for success.* Very Well Mind. https://www.verywellmind.com/what-is-self-esteem-2795868#:~:text=Why%20Self%2DEsteem%20Is%20Important

Clarke, J. (2021). *What is Gestalt Therapy?* Very Well Mind. https://www.verywellmind.com/what-is-gestalt-therapy-4584583

Editorial Team, B. (2023, September 27). *What is shadow psychology?* Better Help. https://www.betterhelp.com/advice/psychologists/what-is-shadow-psychology

*Emotional intelligence.* (2019). Psychology Today. https://www.psychologytoday.com/intl/basics/emotional-intelligence

Heyn, S. (2020, September 3). *Exactly how to do shadow work (an easy 6-step process).* Soul Scroll Journals. https://soulscrolljournals.com/blogs/news/exactly-how-to-do-shadow-work-an-easy-6-step-process

Hussain, S. (2020, June 21). *Ken Wilber's 3-2-1 process: A method for retracting shadow projections.* Ox-Head Psychology. https://oxheadpsychology.com.au/ken-wilbers-3-2-1-process-a-method-for-retracting-shadow-projections

Jeffrey, S. (2019, April 15). *Shadow work: A complete guide to getting to know your darker half.* Scott Jeffrey. https://scottjeffrey.com/shadow-work

Lamkin, W. A. (2020, August 24). *The mandala: An archetype of the self.* Medium. https://medium.com/@WilliamLamkin/the-mandala-an-archetype-of-the-self-72c30146d39d

LaVine, R. (2023, March 28). *100+ deep shadow work prompts to accept yourself and move forward.* Science of People. https://www.scienceofpeople.com/shadow-work-prompts/#:~:text=Shadow%20work%20prompts%20for%20inner%2Dchild%20healing

Lewis, J. (2023, July 29). *Shadow self: What is it and how can it help you?* Zella Life. https://www.zellalife.com/blog/shadow-self-what-is-it-and-how-can-it-help-you/

Lopes, C. (2020, June 9). *What is shadow work?* YouTube. https://www.youtube.com/watch?v=5kDN7g9kBAs&t=8s

Maria. (2021, January 4). *19 top reasons why self-discovery is important.* Aim Lief. https://aimlief.com/why-is-self-discovery-so-important/

McKenna, K. (2023, June 11). *Why naming your feelings matters*. Sit With Kelly. https://www.sitwithkelly.com/blog/feelings

Mind. (2019). *Tips to improve your self-esteem*. Mind. https://www.mind.org.uk/information-support/types-of-mental-health-problems/self-esteem/tips-to-improve-your-self-esteem

*100 self-love affirmations for higher self-esteem*. (2021, April 20). Gratitude Blog. https://blog.gratefulness.me/20-affirmations-to-say-to-yourself-when-you-need-support

Pahwa, V. (2023, January 1). *50 nothing comes easy quotes to deeply love hard work*. Uprise High. https://uprisehigh.com/build-yourself/nothing-comes-easy-quotes

Raypole, C. (2020, March 31). *Repressed emotions: finding and releasing them*. Healthline. https://www.healthline.com/health/repressed-emotions

Riopel, L. (2019, September 14). *17 self-awareness activities and exercises*. Positive Psychology. https://positivepsychology.com/self-awareness-exercises-activities-test

*6 steps toward emotional mastery*. (n.d.). Skills You Need. https://www.skillsyouneed.com/rhubarb/emotional-mastery.html#:~:text=Emotional%20mastery%20is%20the%20gradual

Solis-Moreira, J. (2022, August 12). *6 ways to practice self-love*. Forbes Health. https://www.forbes.com/health/mind/how-to-practice-self-love/

*3-2-1 process for the shadow* (n.d.). Bhavana Learning Group. https://bhavanalearninggroup.com/wp-content/uploads/321-Process-for-the-Shadow.pdf

Williams, K. (2022, May 16). *35 shadow work prompts for self-love*. KB in Bloom. https://kbinbloom.com/shadow-work-prompts-for-self-love/#:~:text=Deeper%20Self%2DLove%20Shadow%20Work%20Prompts%3A&text=Write%20down%20how%20you%20believe

Wooll, M. (2022, June 13). *8 benefits of shadow work and how to start practicing It*. BetterUp. https://www.betterup.com/blog/shadow-work

Work, I. S. (2021, October 13). *30 shadow work prompts for self-worth*. Inner Shadow Work. https://innershadowwork.com/shadow-work-prompts-for-self-worth/References

Subscribe To Sofia Visconti
As a subscriber you will receive a Free Gift + You wil be the first to hear about new books, articles and more exclusives just for you

[CLICK HERE](#)

www.ingramcontent.com/pod-product-compliance
Lightning Source LLC
Chambersburg PA
CBHW072005150726
47999CB00002B/515